ACTION MATHS

2nd CLASS

FOLENS

Introduction to teachers and parents

Action Maths has been developed by a team of experienced primary teachers and consultants in accordance with the aims and objectives of the revised Primary School Curriculum and the accompanying Teacher Guidelines.

The series underpins the key areas of:

- use of concrete materials
- development and correct use of mathematical language
- real life problem solving
- cooperative group work
- oral maths
- estimation
- written computation
- integration with other subjects.

Action Maths is a creative new maths series that aims to equip children for the 21st century.

Consultants

Valerie O'Dowd and Ena Fitzpatrick

Authors

Clifford Brown (6th), Denis Courtney (5th), Liam Gaynor (3rd & 4th),
Trina Cooney (3rd), Thérèse Dooley (2nd), Francis Connolly (1st), Yvonne Keating (1st),
Angela Curley (Senior Infants), Jacqueline O'Donohoe (Senior Infants),
Deirdre Whelan (Junior Infants)

Editor: Deirdre Whelan
Cover & Book Design: Philip Ryan
Cover illustration: Charlie-Ann Turner
Illustration: Carol Kearns, Martin Pierce, Kate Walsh
ISBN 0 86121 949 X

© Folens Publishers 2002

Hibernian Industrial Estate, Greenhills Road, Tallaght, Dublin 24
Produced by Folens Publishers

CONTENTS

This symbol denotes the inclusion of an appropriate photocopiable sheet in the accompanying Teacher's Manual.

A **How many?**

B **Draw a picture of your classroom. Ask your friend questions about it.**

A Write an estimate and an amount for **each** set.

Estimate   Amount

A Draw 12 pencils.

Draw 14 apples.

B Draw 17 sweets.

Draw 13 biscuits.

C Draw 19 buttons.

Draw 15 leaves.

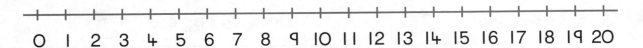

0 1 2 3 4 5 6 7 8 9 10 11 12 13 14 15 16 17 18 19 20

A What number comes **after**?

| 8 | 9 | | 10 | | | 14 | | | 13 | | | 19 | |

| 16 | | | 15 | | | 11 | | | 18 | | | 12 | |

B What number comes **before**?

| 6 | 7 | | 11 | | 20 | | 10 | | 17 |

| 15 | | 13 | | 12 | | 18 | | 19 |

C What number comes **between**?

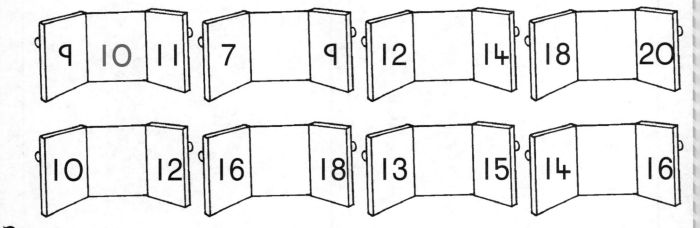

| 9 | 10 | 11 | 7 | | 9 | 12 | | 14 | 18 | | 20 |

| 10 | | 12 | 16 | | 18 | 13 | | 15 | 14 | | 16 |

```
+---+---+---+---+---+---+---+---+---+---+---+---+---+---+---+---+---+---+---+---+---+
0   1   2   3   4   5   6   7   8   9   10  11  12  13  14  15  16  17  18  19  20
```

A Add.

☐ + ☐ = ☐

☐ + ☐ = ☐

☐ + ☐ = ☐

☐ + ☐ = ☐

☐ + ☐ = ☐

☐ + ☐ = ☐

☐ + ☐ = ☐

☐ + ☐ = ☐

☐ + ☐ = ☐

B Add.

$3 + 4 =$ ☐ $4 + 3 =$ ☐ $5 + 6 =$ ☐ $7 + 4 =$ ☐

$8 + 3 =$ ☐ $9 + 5 =$ ☐ $6 + 7 =$ ☐ $7 + 5 =$ ☐

$4 + 2 =$ ☐ $5 + 4 =$ ☐ $6 + 5 =$ ☐ $8 + 4 =$ ☐

$7 + 3 =$ ☐ $9 + 6 =$ ☐ $10 + 8 =$ ☐ $8 + 7 =$ ☐

0 1 2 3 4 5 6 7 8 9 10 11 12 13 14 15 16 17 18 19 20

A

12 − 3 = ☐

8 − 2 = ☐

10 − 5 = ☐

B

7 − 2 = ☐

13 − 4 = ☐

10 − 3 = ☐

12 − 6 = ☐

9 − 4 = ☐

14 − 5 = ☐

C Try these. Use links, cubes or the number line.

8 − 2 = ☐   9 − 1 = ☐   12 − 5 = ☐   11 − 2 = ☐

10 − 4 = ☐   14 − 6 = ☐   16 − 8 = ☐   9 − 7 = ☐

12 − 7 = ☐   13 − 5 = ☐   10 − 8 = ☐   18 − 9 = ☐

11 − 3 = ☐   11 − 5 = ☐   15 − 8 = ☐   17 − 9 = ☐

A Use colours to make your own patterns.

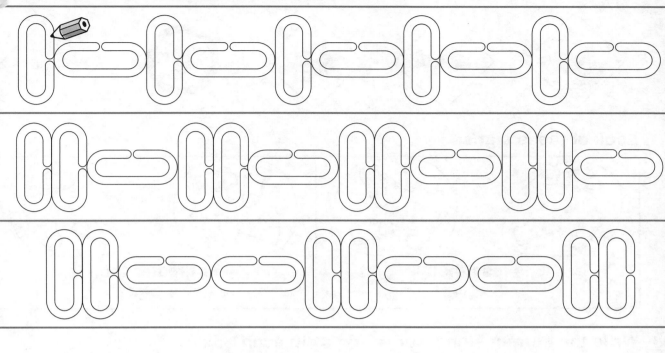

A What do these signs mean?

Look at these signs.

3 is less than 4
3 < 4

4 is greater than 3
4 > 3

B Write the correct sign > or < or = in each box.

 ☐     ☐

 ☐    ☐

C Write > or < between these numbers.

3 < 5	5 ☐ 8	6 ☐ 9
4 ☐ 8	7 ☐ 5	15 ☐ 19
6 ☐ 4	17 ☐ 18	19 ☐ 18
12 ☐ 7	5 ☐ 2	9 ☐ 7
3 ☐ 13	12 ☐ 10	9 ☐ 10
7 ☐ 6	11 ☐ 1	16 ☐ 17

A

3 + 1 = ☐

1 + 3 = ☐

4 + 2 = ☐

2 + 4 = ☐

B Add and colour.

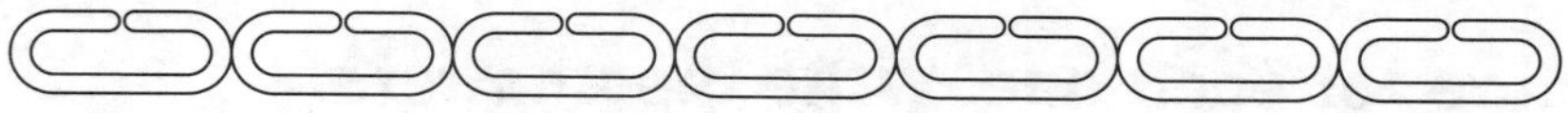

6 + 1 = ☐

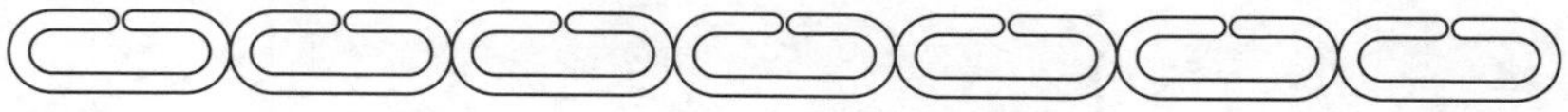

1 + 6 = ☐

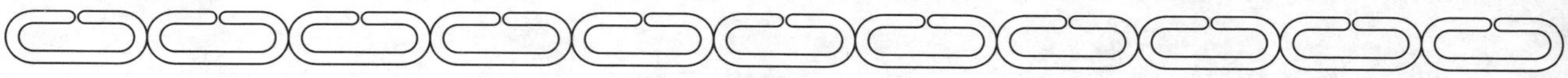

7 + 4 = ☐

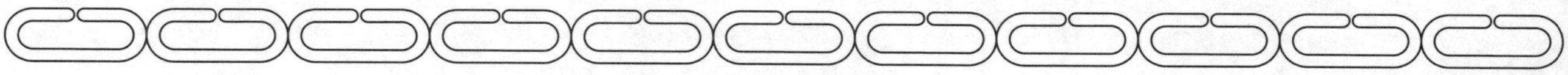

4 + 7 = ☐

C Use your links to do these.

5 + 2 = 2 + ☐   8 + 1 = 1 + ☐   6 + 3 = 3 + ☐

7 + 3 = 3 + ☐   9 + 2 = 2 + ☐   8 + 7 = 7 + ☐

8 + 4 = ☐ + 8   6 + 5 = ☐ + 6   10 + 2 = ☐ + 10

5 + 4 = ☐ + 5   9 + 1 = ☐ + 9   10 + 7 = ☐ + 10

A Tell each story. Write the answers.

 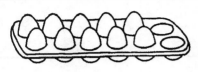 

$3 + 4 =$ ☐ $12 - 2 =$ ☐ $8 - 5 =$ ☐

B Draw a picture for each one. Write the answers.

$5 + 6 =$ ☐ $9 + 4 =$ ☐ $12 - 6 =$ ☐

$8 + 5 =$ ☐ $13 - 6 =$ ☐ $5 + 7 =$ ☐

C Draw pictures for these number sentences.

1. $5 + 6 = 11$ 2. $7 - 4 = 3$ 3. $9 + 7 = 16$

4. $13 + 4 = 17$ 5. $15 - 8 = 7$ 6. $13 - 9 = 4$

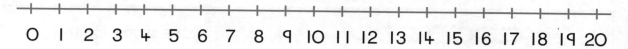

0 1 2 3 4 5 6 7 8 9 10 11 12 13 14 15 16 17 18 19 20

A Write the answers.

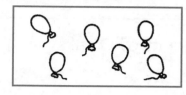 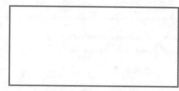 

6   +   **0**   =   ▢

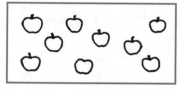 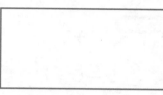 

9   +   **0**   =   ▢

 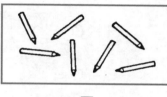 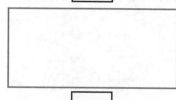

0   +   **7**   =   ▢

B Draw your own pictures.

8   +   **0**   =   ▢

 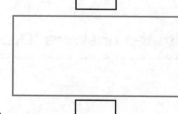

0   +   **5**   =   ▢

C Write the answers.

2 + 0 = ▢   4 + 0 = ▢   7 + 0 = ▢   5 + 0 = ▢

0 + 3 = ▢   0 + 10 = ▢   0 + 8 = ▢   0 + 4 = ▢

15

A

Take away O links.

$3 - 0 = \boxed{}$

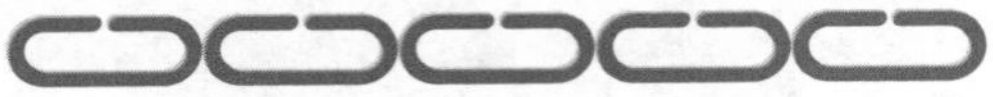

Take away O links.

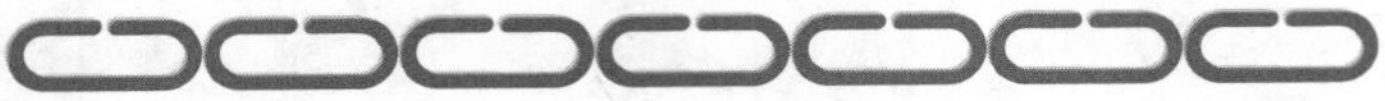

$7 - 0 = \boxed{}$

Take away O links.

$5 - 0 = \boxed{}$

B Try these. Use links.

$2 - 0 = \boxed{}$ $9 - 0 = \boxed{}$ $6 - 0 = \boxed{}$

$4 - 0 = \boxed{}$ $8 - 0 = \boxed{}$ $10 - 0 = \boxed{}$

C Write the answers.

$5 - 5 = \boxed{}$ $3 - 3 = \boxed{}$

D Write the answers. Draw your own pictures.

$7 - 7 = \boxed{}$ $2 - 2 = \boxed{}$

A Join the dots from 1 to 20. Find a dinosaur!

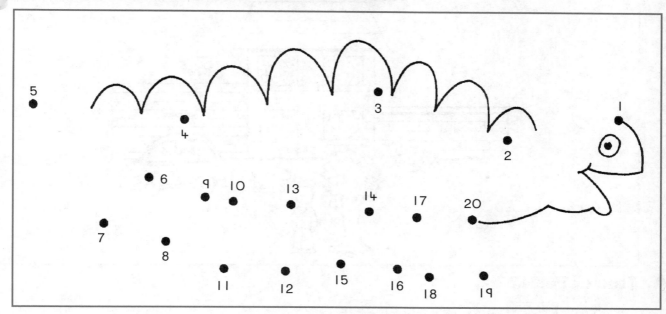

B Join the pairs of numbers that match each total.

Total: 10   Total: 15   Total: 12

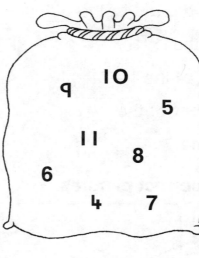

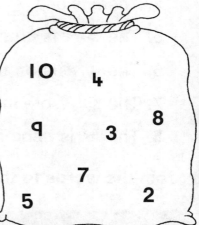

C Fill in + or − for each one.

1. 1 ☐ 4 = 5   4. 11 ☐ 8 = 3

2. 3 ☐ 5 = 8   5. 2 ☐ 2 ☐ 2 = 6

3. 10 ☐ 1 = 9   6. 4 ☐ 4 ☐ 1 = 7

A **True** or **False**?

1. The ▭ is **to the right of** the 🏠 . _____

2. The 🌳 is **between** the 🐕 and the 🚗 . _____

3. The 🚗 is **above** the ▭ . _____

4. There is a 🪟 **to the left of** the ▯ . _____

5. The 🕊 is **under** the 🏠 . _____

6. The 🐱 is **on top of** the ▭ . _____

7. The 🌸 are **in front of** the 🧱 . _____

8. The 🌳 is **behind** the 🏠 . _____

B Join the words to the correct pictures.

to the left of the bird

under the bridge

above the bridge

to the right of the bird

A

5 + 1 = ☐   9 + 1 = ☐   1 + 1 = ☐   3 + 1 = ☐

1 + 4 = ☐   1 + 7 = ☐   1 + 8 = ☐   1 + 6 = ☐

B

2 − 1 = ☐   4 − 1 = ☐   9 − 1 = ☐   8 − 1 = ☐

10 − 1 = ☐   3 − 1 = ☐   6 − 1 = ☐   1 − 1 = ☐

C

1 + 2 = ☐   9 + 2 = ☐   2 + 7 = ☐   2 + 4 = ☐

5 + 2 = ☐   10 + 2 = ☐   8 + 2 = ☐   2 + 6 = ☐

D

3 − 2 = ☐   6 − 2 = ☐   9 − 2 = ☐   11 − 2 = ☐

2 − 2 = ☐   12 − 2 = ☐   5 − 2 = ☐   7 − 2 = ☐

E

1   +1   ☐   +2   ☐   +1   ☐   +2   ☐   +2   ☐

F

2   +2   ☐   +2   ☐   +1   ☐   +1   ☐   +2   ☐

G

10   +2   ☐   +2   ☐   +2   ☐   +2   ☐   +2   ☐

19

10 **units** can be swapped for 1 **ten** like this:

A Draw the swaps that can be made for these units.
The first one is done for you.

1.

   = | Tens | Units | | |
|---|---|---|---|
| 1 | 4 | = | 14 |

2.

   = | Tens | Units | | |
|---|---|---|---|
| | | = | |

3.

   = | Tens | Units | | |
|---|---|---|---|
| | | = | |

4.

   = | Tens | Units | | |
|---|---|---|---|
| | | = | |

A Draw the swaps that can be made for these units.

1.

 = [ ] = Tens [ ] Units [ ] = [ ]

2.

 = [ ] = Tens [ ] Units [ ] = [ ]

3.

 = [ ] = Tens [ ] Units [ ] = [ ]

4.

 = [ ] = Tens [ ] Units [ ] = [ ]

5.

 = [ ] = Tens [ ] Units [ ] = [ ]

A **P** Show these numbers on your place-value boards. Write the numbers.

1.
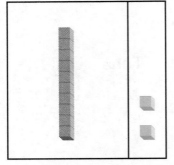
T U
=

2.
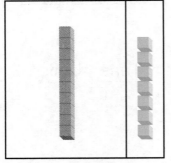
T U
=

3.
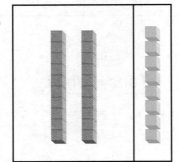
T U
=

4.
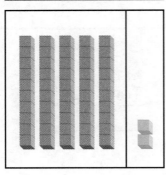
T U
=

5.
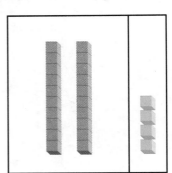
T U
=

6.
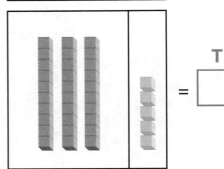
T U
=

7.
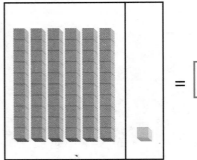
T U
=

8.
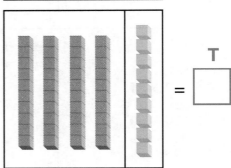
T U
=

B Try these.

	T	U
26 =	2	6

	T	U
20 =		

	T	U
15 =		

	T	U
39 =		

	T	U
4 =		

	T	U
9 =		

	T	U
50 =		

	T	U
10 =		

A **P** Show these numbers on your place-value boards. Write the numbers.

1.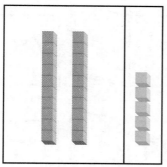

T U
= □ □

5.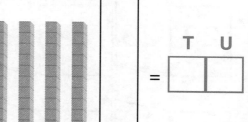

T U
= □ □

2.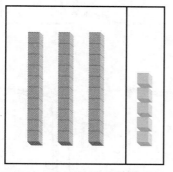

T U
= □ □

6.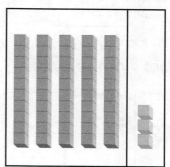

T U
= □ □

3.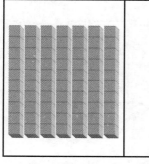

T U
= □ □

7.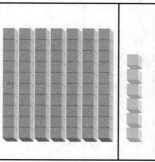

T U
= □ □

4.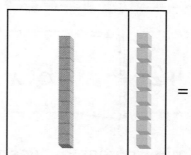

T U
= □ □

8.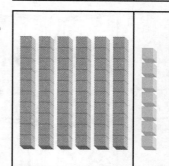

T U
= □ □

B Try these.

	T	U			T	U			T	U			T	U
35 =	3	5		41 =				28 =				16 =		

	T	U			T	U			T	U			T	U
56 =				38 =				60 =				32 =		

A What number comes **after**?

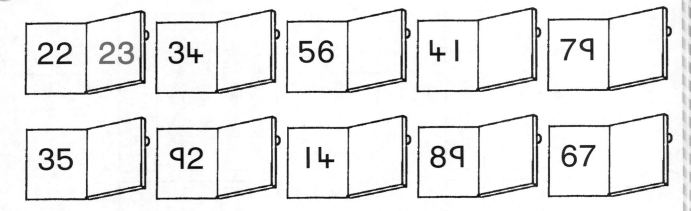

22 | 23   34 | ___   56 | ___   41 | ___   79 | ___

35 | ___   92 | ___   14 | ___   89 | ___   67 | ___

B What number comes **before**?

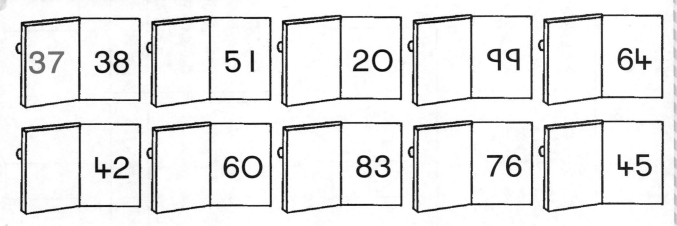

37 | 38   ___ | 51   ___ | 20   ___ | 99   ___ | 64

___ | 42   ___ | 60   ___ | 83   ___ | 76   ___ | 45

C What number comes **between**?

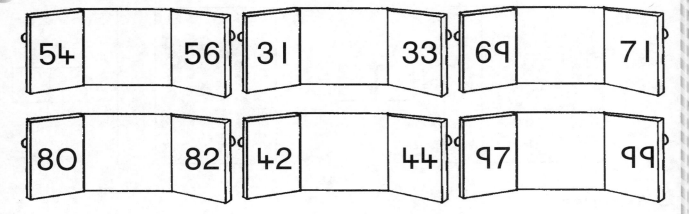

54 | ___ | 56   31 | ___ | 33   69 | ___ | 71

80 | ___ | 82   42 | ___ | 44   97 | ___ | 99

D What number comes **before** and **after**?

___ | 21 | ___   ___ | 49 | ___   ___ | 30 | ___

A

$4 + 4 = \boxed{}$

$3 + 3 = \boxed{}$

B Try these. Use links to help you.

$3 + 3 = \boxed{}$	$5 + 5 = \boxed{}$	$7 + 7 = \boxed{}$	$8 + 8 = \boxed{}$
$9 + 9 = \boxed{}$	$10 + 10 = \boxed{}$	$8 - 4 = \boxed{}$	$6 - 3 = \boxed{}$
$14 - 7 = \boxed{}$	$16 - 8 = \boxed{}$	$20 - 10 = \boxed{}$	$18 - 9 = \boxed{}$
$6 + 6 = \boxed{}$	$14 - 7 = \boxed{}$	$10 - 5 = \boxed{}$	$12 - 6 = \boxed{}$

C

$4 + 3 = \boxed{}$

$6 + 5 = \boxed{}$

D Try these. Use links to help you.

$5 + 6 = \boxed{}$	$7 + 6 = \boxed{}$	$8 + 7 = \boxed{}$	$9 + 8 = \boxed{}$
$10 + 9 = \boxed{}$	$7 - 4 = \boxed{}$	$11 - 5 = \boxed{}$	$13 - 7 = \boxed{}$
$15 - 7 = \boxed{}$	$17 - 8 = \boxed{}$	$19 - 9 = \boxed{}$	$15 - 8 = \boxed{}$
$17 - 9 = \boxed{}$	$13 - 6 = \boxed{}$	$11 - 6 = \boxed{}$	$9 - 4 = \boxed{}$

A Match the shape to its name.

cuboid

cone

cube

cylinder

sphere

B Copy and colour these 3-D shapes.

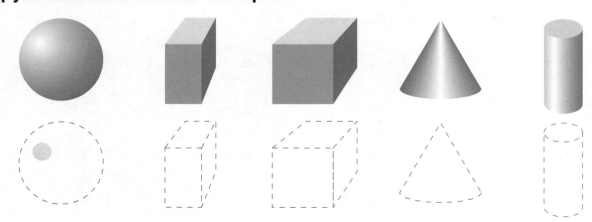

A **How many corners, faces and edges do these shapes have?**

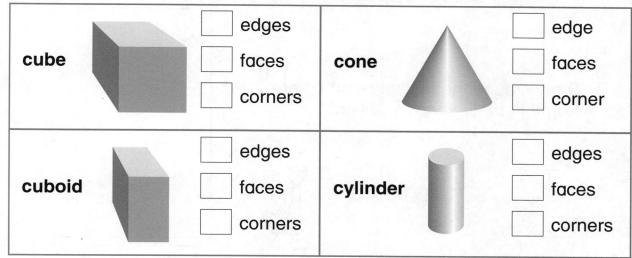

cube — ☐ edges ☐ faces ☐ corners

cone — ☐ edge ☐ faces ☐ corner

cuboid — ☐ edges ☐ faces ☐ corners

cylinder — ☐ edges ☐ faces ☐ corners

B **Match.**

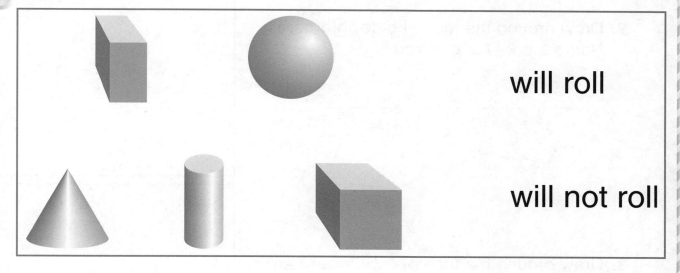

will roll

will not roll

C **Match.**

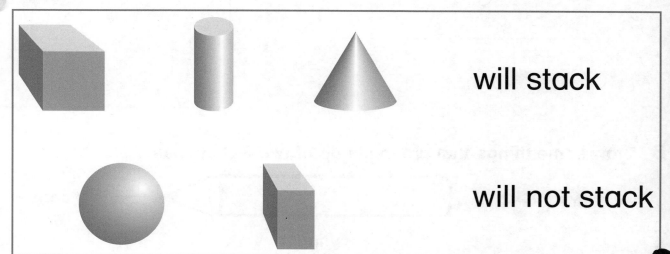

will stack

will not stack

A **To do.**

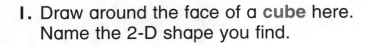

1. Draw around the face of a **cube** here. Name the 2-D shape you find.

S

2. Draw around the face of a **cuboid** here. Name the 2-D shape you find.

_____

3. Draw around the face of a **cylinder** here. Name the 2-D shape you find.

_____

B **Draw some things that are made up of two 3-D shapes.**

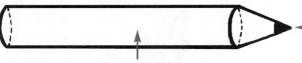

e.g. Pencil

cone

cylinder

28

A **Can you find these shapes in the classroom?**

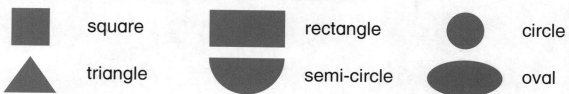

square ■ rectangle circle

triangle semi-circle oval

1. Which shapes have **straight** edges? _____

2. Which shapes have **curved** edges? _____

B **Colour. Use the code below.**

green black pink red blue yellow

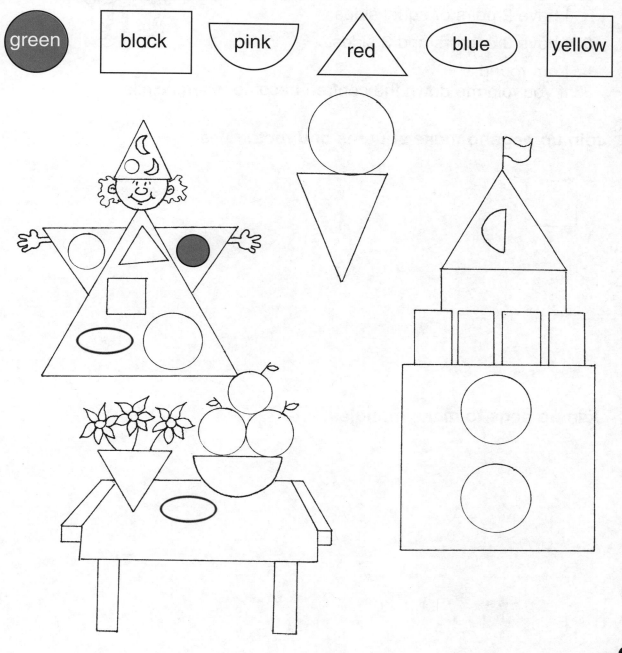

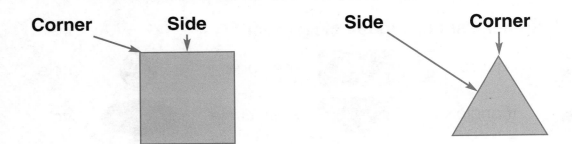

Corner   Side   Side   Corner

A What is my name? Draw me in your copy.

1. I have **4** corners and **4** sides.
   My sides are all the same length.

2. I have **4** corners and **4** sides.
   I have **2** pairs of equal sides.

3. I have **3** corners and **3** sides.

4. I am round.
   If you fold me down the centre I become a semi-circle.

B Join up pegs to make squares and rectangles.

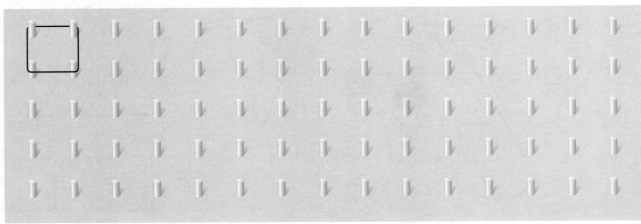

C Join up pegs to make triangles.

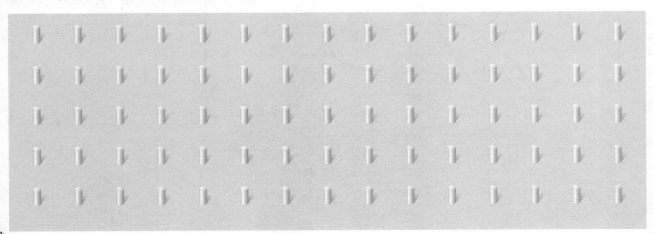

TEN

A Each pair of cards add up to ten. Fill in the blank cards.

B Each set of cards add up to ten. Fill in the blank cards.

C Try these. Use links to help you.

10 + 2 = ☐   10 + 4 = ☐   10 + 7 = ☐   10 + 8 = ☐

10 + 9 = ☐   11 − 1 = ☐   13 − 3 = ☐   15 − 5 = ☐

17 − 7 = ☐   16 − 6 = ☐   14 − 4 = ☐   18 − 8 = ☐

A Write.

1. 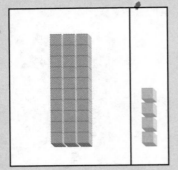 = [T][U]

3. 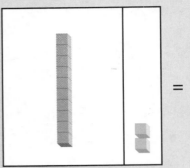 = [T][U]

2. 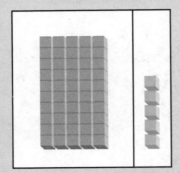 = [T][U]

4. 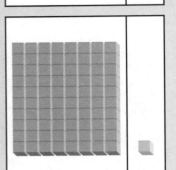 = [T][U]

B Where are the letters?

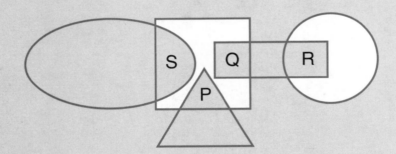

The letter **P** is in the triangle △ and the square ☐.

The letter **Q** is in the _____ and the _____.

The letter **R** is in the _____ and the _____.

The letter **S** is in the _____ and the _____.

C Fill in the boxes.

1. ☐ + ☐ = 8   **2.** ☐ + ☐ = 10   **3.** ☐ + ☐ = 13

4. ☐ + ☐ = 15   **5.** ☐ + ☐ = 17   **6.** ☐ + ☐ = 19

A **1.**

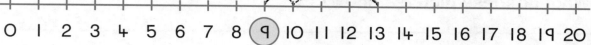

O 1 2 3 4 5 6 7 8 ⑨ 10 11 12 13 14 15 16 17 18 19 20

$9 + 4 = \boxed{}$

2.

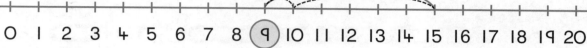

O 1 2 3 4 5 6 7 8 ⑨ 10 11 12 13 14 15 16 17 18 19 20

$9 + 6 = \boxed{}$

3.

O 1 2 3 4 5 6 7 ⑧ 9 10 11 12 13 14 15 16 17 18 19 20

$8 + 4 = \boxed{}$

4.

O 1 2 3 4 5 6 7 ⑧ 9 10 11 12 13 14 15 16 17 18 19 20

$8 + 3 = \boxed{}$

B **Try these.**

1. $9 + 3 = \boxed{}$ $9 + 5 = \boxed{}$ $9 + 7 = \boxed{}$ $9 + 8 = \boxed{}$

$9 + 9 = \boxed{}$ $8 + 5 = \boxed{}$ $8 + 6 = \boxed{}$ $8 + 7 = \boxed{}$

2. $11 - 9 = \boxed{}$ $13 - 9 = \boxed{}$ $16 - 9 = \boxed{}$ $14 - 9 = \boxed{}$

$17 - 9 = \boxed{}$ $13 - 8 = \boxed{}$ $11 - 8 = \boxed{}$ $14 - 8 = \boxed{}$

3. $12 - 3 = \boxed{}$ $14 - 5 = \boxed{}$ $17 - 8 = \boxed{}$ $15 - 6 = \boxed{}$

$13 - 4 = \boxed{}$ $12 - 4 = \boxed{}$ $14 - 6 = \boxed{}$ $11 - 3 = \boxed{}$

A What do these pictures show?

(2 + ☐) + ☐

(3 + ☐) + ☐

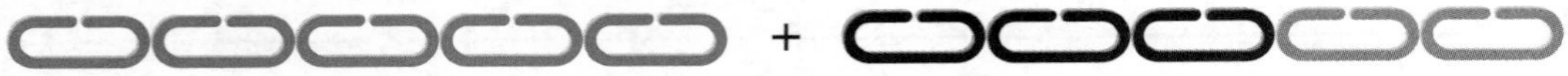

☐ + (☐ + ☐)

(☐ + ☐) + ☐

(☐ + ☐) + ☐

☐ + (☐ + ☐)

B Use your links to do these.

(8 + 3) + 4 = ☐   6 + (4 + 7) = ☐   5 + (1 + 6) = ☐

(4 + 3) + 9 = ☐   6 + (3 + 2) = ☐   (6 + 3) + 2 = ☐

7 + (1 + 9) = ☐   (2 + 4) + 5 = ☐   1 + (6 + 7) = ☐

(9 + 4) + 6 = ☐   (8 + 5) + 4 = ☐   (7 + 6) + 5 = ☐

A

(1 + 5) + 3 = ☐

1 + (5 + 3) = ☐

(3 + 2) + 4 = ☐

3 + (2 + 4) = ☐

B What does this picture show? Write the missing numerals.

(1 + ☐) + ☐ = ☐

☐ + (2 + ☐) = ☐

C Use links to do these.

(2 + 4) + 6 = ☐   (5 + 5) + 8 = ☐

2 + (4 + 6) = ☐   5 + (5 + 8) = ☐

(8 + 1) + 4 = ☐   6 + (5 + 7) = ☐

8 + (1 + 4) = ☐   (6 + 5) + 7 = ☐

D Write the answers.

1. 3 + (4 + 7) = 3 + ☐ = ☐   2. (6 + 6) + 5 = ☐ + 5 = ☐

   (3 + 4) + 7 = ☐ + 7 = ☐   6 + (6 + 5) = 6 + ☐ = ☐

A **Write the number sentence for each story.**

1. Jim has **7** cards. He finds **5** cards. How many cards has he now?

2. Sarah saw **8** copies on one table. She saw **6** copies on another table. How many copies did she see?

3. There were 12 grapes in a box. Paul ate 5 of them. How many grapes were left?

4. Joe is **10** years old. Beth is **3** years older than Joe. How old is Beth?

B **Write or draw stories for these number sentences.**

$3 + 5 = 8$	$6 + 7 = 13$
$7 - 4 = 3$	$10 - 8 = 2$

C **Write word sentences for these number sentences.**

$5 + 8 = \boxed{}$ $6 + 7 = \boxed{}$ $3 + 5 = \boxed{}$ $4 + 6 = \boxed{}$

$13 - 9 = \boxed{}$ $14 - 8 = \boxed{}$ $12 - 11 = \boxed{}$ $18 - 5 = \boxed{}$

A Add the numbers on the dice faces.

☐ + ☐ + ☐ = ☐   ☐ + ☐ + ☐ = ☐

☐ + ☐ + ☐ = ☐   ☐ + ☐ + ☐ = ☐

☐ + ☐ + ☐ = ☐   ☐ + ☐ + ☐ = ☐

B Draw the dots on the dice faces.

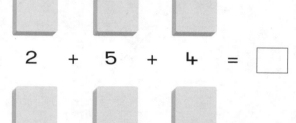

2 + 5 + 4 = ☐   4 + 5 + 4 = ☐

1 + 6 + 2 = ☐   3 + 4 + 5 = ☐

C Use the number line to add these numbers.

0 1 2 3 4 5 6 7 8 9 10 11 12 13 14 15 16 17 18 19 20

4 + 5 + 3 = ☐   7 + 1 + 8 = ☐   3 + 5 + 9 = ☐

9 + 5 + 4 = ☐   6 + 9 + 3 = ☐   2 + 3 + 8 = ☐

2 + 8 + 4 = ☐   3 + 7 + 6 = ☐   5 + 6 + 5 = ☐

D Fill in the boxes to get the correct answer.

1. ☐ + ☐ + ☐ = 6   3. ☐ + ☐ + ☐ = 9

2. ☐ + ☐ + ☐ = 8   4. ☐ + ☐ + ☐ = 10

A half is written like this: $\frac{1}{2}$

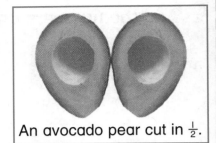

An avocado pear cut in $\frac{1}{2}$.

A Shade in $\frac{1}{2}$ of each of these shapes.

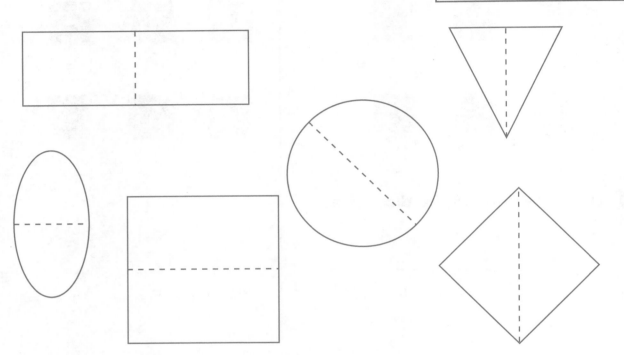

B Draw the other half of each of these shapes.

A **For each of these shapes write whether the shaded part is:**

About a half	More than a half	Less than a half

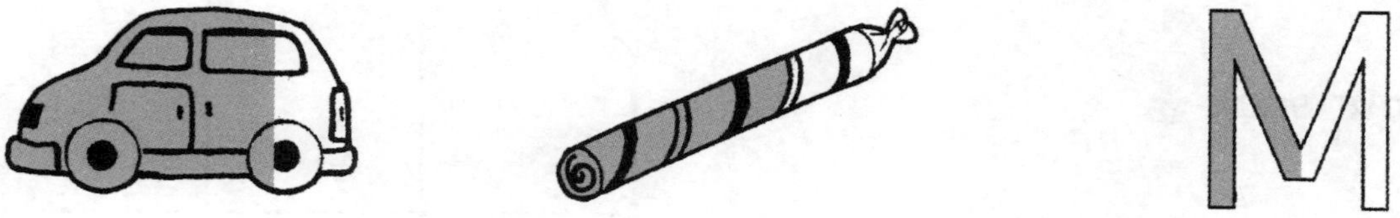

B **Draw the other half of these pictures.**

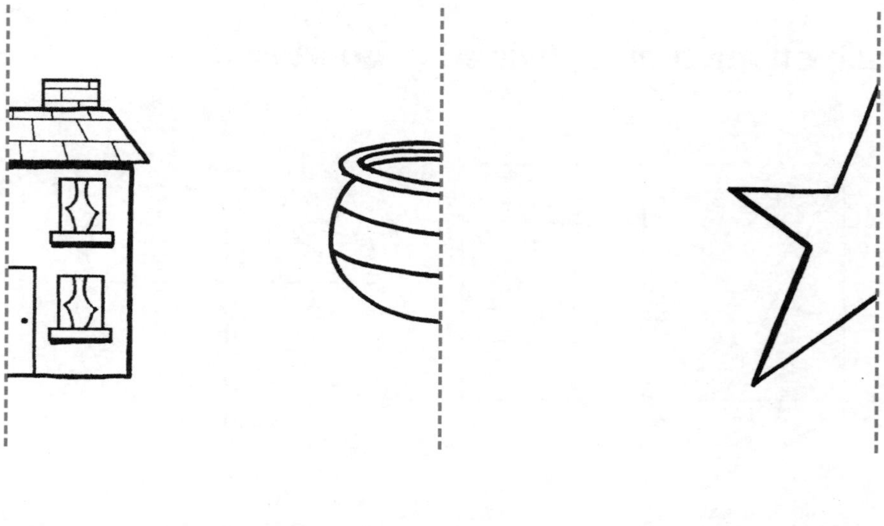

There are **4** children.
There is only one bar of chocolate.
What will Mum do?

The bar is broken into
4 equal parts.
Each part is a **quarter**.

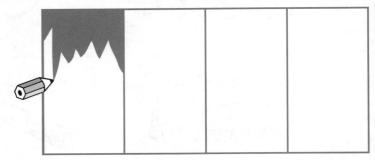

A Colour each $\frac{1}{4}$.

A quarter is written like this: $\frac{1}{4}$

B Colour $\frac{1}{4}$ of each of these shapes. One is done for you.

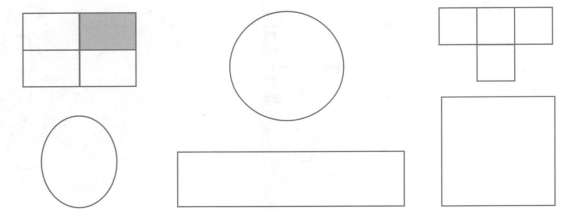

C Colour each shape that is divided in quarters.

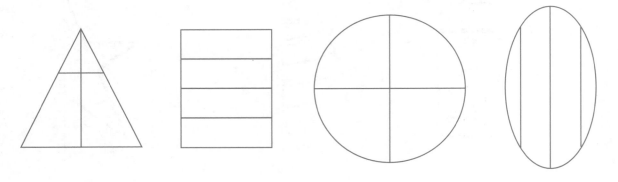

A Look at each shape. How many **equal parts** do you see?
How many equal parts are shaded?

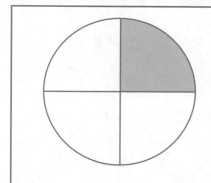
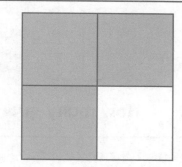
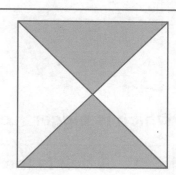

I see ☐ equal parts.   I see ☐ equal parts.   I see ☐ equal parts.

☐ part is shaded.   ☐ parts are shaded.   ☐ parts are shaded.

B

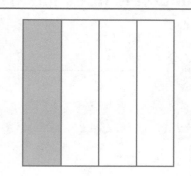
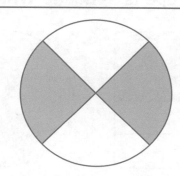
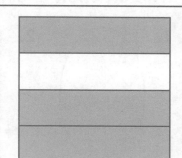

I see ☐ equal parts.   I see ☐ equal parts.   I see ☐ equal parts.

☐ part is shaded.   ☐ parts are shaded.   ☐ parts are shaded.

☐ parts are not shaded.   ☐ parts are not shaded.   ☐ part is not shaded.

C What **fraction** of each object is **missing**?

   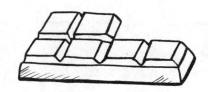

A

Which is bigger $\frac{1}{2}$ or $\frac{1}{4}$? ☐ How many **quarters** make a **half**? ☐

A **half** is the same as **two quarters**.

	$\frac{1}{4}$
$\frac{1}{2}$	$\frac{1}{4}$

B What fraction of each shape is shaded? What fraction is not shaded?

1.

2.

3.

4.

$\boxed{\frac{1}{2}}$ is shaded. ☐ is shaded. ☐ is shaded. ☐ is shaded.

☐ is not shaded. ☐ is not shaded. ☐ is not shaded. ☐ is not shaded.

C Shade in $\frac{1}{2}$ of each shape below. What **new** shape have you found?
The first one is done for you.

$\frac{1}{2}$ of the ☐
is a △.

A

1. Colour these numbers on the 100 square.
One is done for you.
7, 25, 50, 17, 89, 63, 36, 20, 41, 33, 94, 49, 3.

1	2	3	4	5	6	7	8	9	10
11	12	13	14	15	16	17	18	19	20
21	22	23	24	25	26	27	28	29	30
31	32	33	34	35	36	37	38	39	40
41	42	43	44	45	46	47	48	49	50
51	52	53	54	55	56	57	58	59	60
61	62	63	64	65	66	67	68	69	70
71	72	73	74	75	76	77	78	79	80
81	82	83	84	85	86	87	88	89	90
91	92	93	94	95	96	97	98	99	100

Row → (points to row 51–60)

Column ↑ (points to column 8)

2. Write all the numbers in row 6.

☐ ☐ ☐ ☐ ☐
☐ ☐ ☐ ☐ ☐

3. Write all the numbers in column 8.

☐ ☐ ☐ ☐ ☐
☐ ☐ ☐ ☐ ☐

4. Write all the numbers ending with 7.

| 17 | ☐ | ☐ | ☐ | ☐ | ☐ | ☐ | ☐ | ☐ |

5. Write all the numbers beginning with 7.

☐ ☐ ☐ ☐ ☐ ☐ ☐ ☐ ☐ ☐

B

Start at   **5.**   Go **forward**   **3.**   You are at ☐ .

Start at   **16.**   Go **forward**   **5.**   You are at ☐ .

Start at   **52.**   Go **forward**   **9.**   You are at ☐ .

Start at   **11.**   Go **back**   **5.**   You are at ☐ .

Start at   **36.**   Go **back**   **8.**   You are at ☐ .

Start at   **65.**   Go **back**   **6.**   You are at ☐ .

C These are parts of the 100 square. Write in the **missing** numbers.

| 2 | | 4 | |

| | 35 | | |

7	
17	

61	
81	

20	
30	

| 12 | |
| 22 | |

| 56 | | |
| | 67 | |

| 71 | | |
| | | 83 |

43

A

Start at **24**. Go **forward 5**.
Write the number.

Start at **31**. Go **forward 10**.
Write the number.

Start at **7**. Go **forward 20**.
Write the number.

Start at **68**. Go **back 10**.
Write the number.

Start at **94**. Go **back 30**.
Write the number.

1	2	3	4	5	6	7	8	9	10
11	12	13	14	15	16	17	18	19	20
21	22	23	24	25	26	27	28	29	30
31	32	33	34	35	36	37	38	39	40
41	42	43	44	45	46	47	48	49	50
51	52	53	54	55	56	57	58	59	60
61	62	63	64	65	66	67	68	69	70
71	72	73	74	75	76	77	78	79	80
81	82	83	84	85	86	87	88	89	90
91	92	93	94	95	96	97	98	99	100

B **P** Try these on your 100 square. Look for patterns.
Make more patterns of your own.

$5 + 3 =$

$15 + 3 =$

$25 + 3 =$

$35 + 3 =$

$16 + 5 =$

$26 + 5 =$

$36 + 5 =$

$46 + 5 =$

$7 + 7 =$

$17 + 7 =$

$27 + 7 =$

$37 + 7 =$

$9 + 4 =$

$19 + 4 =$

$29 + 4 =$

$39 + 4 =$

C

$18 - 6 =$

$28 - 6 =$

$38 - 6 =$

$10 - 7 =$

$20 - 7 =$

$30 - 7 =$

$15 - 10 =$

$25 - 10 =$

$35 - 10 =$

$22 - 8 =$

$32 - 8 =$

$42 - 8 =$

D

$4 + 10 =$

$4 + 20 =$

$4 + 10 + 20 =$

$43 + 10 =$

$43 + 30 =$

$43 + 20 + 30 =$

$26 + 10 =$

$26 + 40 =$

$26 + 20 + 10 =$

A Ring each of these numbers on the 1OO square. Colour the nearest 1O. One is done for you.

16, 47, 68, 56, 38, 89, 76, 28, 7.

1	2	3	4	5	6	7	8	9	10
11	12	13	14	15	16	17	18	19	20
21	22	23	24	25	26	27	28	29	30
31	32	33	34	35	36	37	38	39	40
41	42	43	44	45	46	47	48	49	50
51	52	53	54	55	56	57	58	59	60
61	62	63	64	65	66	67	68	69	70
71	72	73	74	75	76	77	78	79	80
81	82	83	84	85	86	87	88	89	90
91	92	93	94	95	96	97	98	99	100

B Write these numbers to the nearest 1O.

> If the number is 5 or if it ends in 5 round it up to the nearest 1O.
> Example: 35 ⟶ 4O

1. 41 [40]   27 [ ]

2. 37 [ ]   62 [ ]   69 [ ]   74 [ ]   81 [ ]

3. 17 [ ]   5 [ ]   86 [ ]   22 [ ]   51 [ ]

4. 71 [ ]   18 [ ]   9 [ ]   19 [ ]   36 [ ]

C Make estimates for these additions.

26 + 23   Estimate [ ]

41 + 37   Estimate [ ]

57 + 32   Estimate [ ]

45 + 12   Estimate [ ]

76 + 11   Estimate [ ]

20 + 29   Estimate [ ]

34 + 24   Estimate [ ]

48 + 42   Estimate [ ]

71 + 16   Estimate [ ]

June collected **24** chestnuts and Ned collected **13** chestnuts.
How many chestnuts did they collect altogether?

24 + 13 = 37

They collected **37** chestnuts between them.

A **Draw or write a story for this sum.**

25 + 14 =

B **Try these. Use Base Ten blocks or Unifix cubes to help you. First make an estimate for each answer.**

1.	25 + 24 =	24 + 41 =	47 + 12 =
2.	56 + 22 =	34 + 44 =	40 + 17 =
3.	64 + 23 =	73 + 16 =	38 + 11 =
4.	52 + 44 =	36 + 22 =	21 + 13 =
5.	50 + 26 =	63 + 32 =	58 + 31 =

C Write your **largest** answer from exercise B here.   Write your **smallest** answer from exercise B here.

A Write the numbers in the coloured boxes.

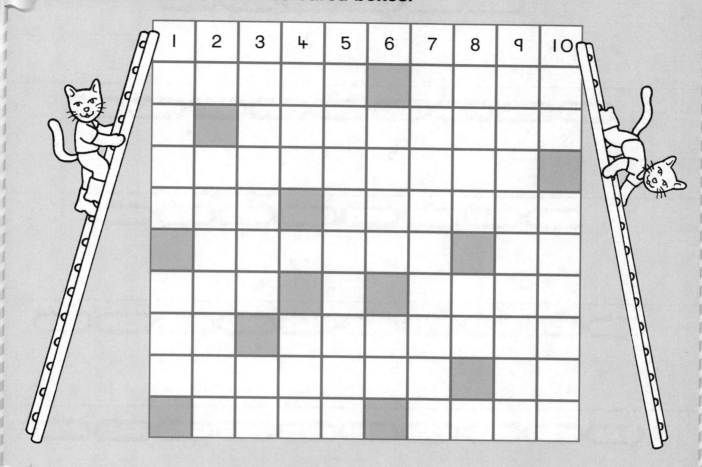

B Match the sums with good estimates.

| 22 + 31 | 51 + 27 | 11 + 78 | 29 + 34 | 46 + 23 |

50   60   70   80   90

C Shade in $\frac{1}{2}$ of this shape.   Shade in $\frac{1}{4}$ of this shape.

ADDING ON

A

$4 + \boxed{} = 6$

$6 + \boxed{} = 9$

$6 + \boxed{} = 8$

$5 + \boxed{} = 10$

$2 + \boxed{} = 10$

B Try these. Use links or cubes to help you.

1. $4 + \boxed{} = 10$ | $8 + \boxed{} = 11$ | $3 + \boxed{} = 8$ | $6 + \boxed{} = 15$

2. $5 + \boxed{} = 10$ | $10 + \boxed{} = 18$ | $5 + \boxed{} = 12$ | $7 + \boxed{} = 15$

3. $9 + \boxed{} = 16$ | $6 + \boxed{} = 14$ | $8 + \boxed{} = 14$ | $6 + \boxed{} = 13$

4. $7 + \boxed{} = 12$ | $9 + \boxed{} = 13$ | $1 + \boxed{} = 10$ | $2 + \boxed{} = 9$

C Write the missing numbers.

$\boxed{} + \boxed{} = 10$ $\boxed{} + \boxed{} = 16$ $\boxed{} + \boxed{} = 19$

A Trace these shapes. Cut them out. Fold them on the dotted line. What do you notice when you fold them?

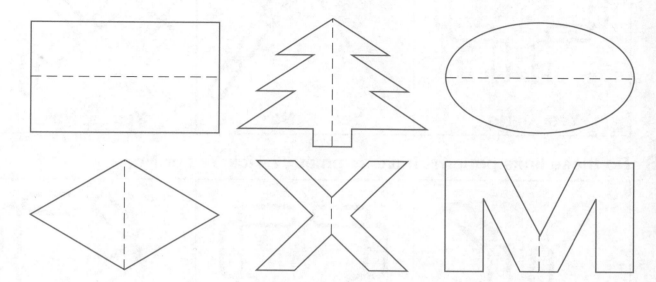

Each of these shapes has **symmetry**.

B Complete these symmetrical shapes.

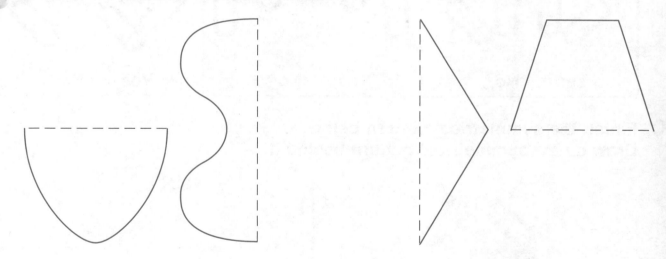

C Draw a line of symmetry through the pictures that have symmetry.

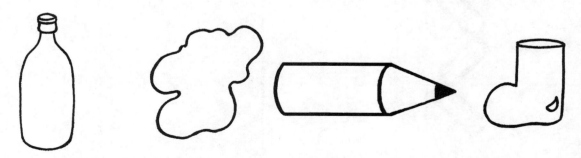

A Do these links patterns have **symmetry**? Tick **Yes** or **No**.

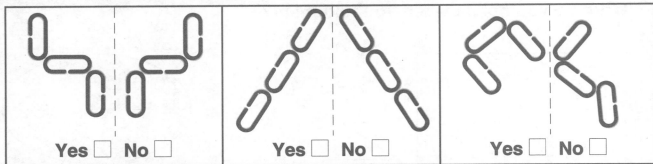

Yes ☐ No ☐   Yes ☐ No ☐   Yes ☐ No ☐

B Do these links patterns have **symmetry**? Tick **Yes** or **No**.

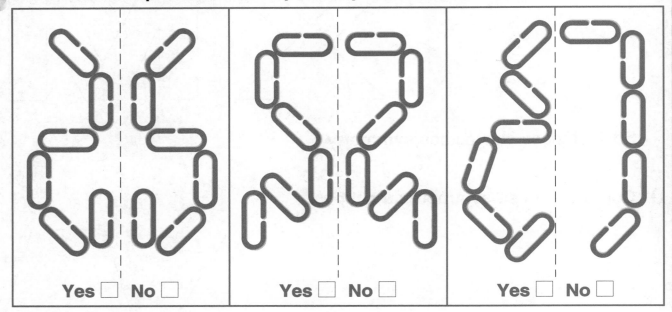

Yes ☐ No ☐   Yes ☐ No ☐   Yes ☐ No ☐

C Finish the symmetrical pattern below.
Draw a new symmetrical pattern beside it.

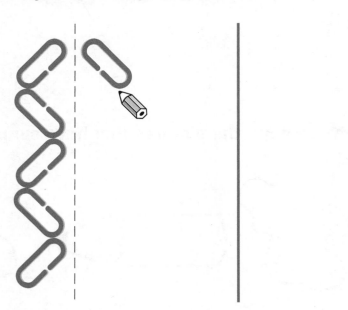

50

A Each shape is half a picture. Put a mirror along each broken line. What do you see? Finish each picture.

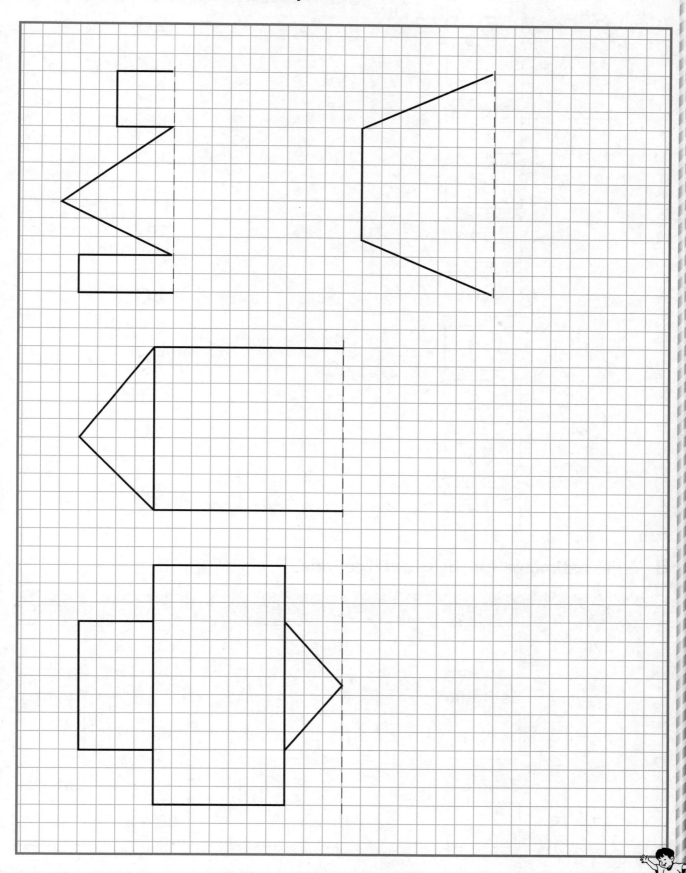

A Match these numbers to the nearest 10.

79	20
51	30
48	40
32	50
27	60
86	70
19	80
43	90
56	
74	

B Write estimates for these subtractions.

	Estimate		Estimate		Estimate
37 – 21		71 – 28		43 – 19	
32 – 18		67 – 13		59 – 29	
27 – 19		32 – 16		86 – 37	

There were
27 pizzas
in the shop.
15 were sold.
How many pizzas
were left?

$27 - 15 = \boxed{12}$

A Draw or write a number sentence for this story.

$24 - 13 = \boxed{}$

B Try these. Use Base Ten blocks or Unifix cubes to help you.

1. $45 - 12 = \boxed{}$ $58 - 22 = \boxed{}$ $39 - 17 = \boxed{}$

   $28 - 23 = \boxed{}$ $56 - 43 = \boxed{}$ $46 - 21 = \boxed{}$

2. $65 - 53 = \boxed{}$ $86 - 41 = \boxed{}$ $78 - 23 = \boxed{}$

   $37 - 12 = \boxed{}$ $29 - 12 = \boxed{}$ $66 - 34 = \boxed{}$

3. $64 - 22 = \boxed{}$ $38 - 18 = \boxed{}$ $27 - 16 = \boxed{}$

   $78 - 57 = \boxed{}$ $80 - 20 = \boxed{}$ $84 - 62 = \boxed{}$

C Write your **biggest** answer from exercise B here. $\boxed{}$ Write your **smallest** answer from exercise B here. $\boxed{}$

53

A These are some of the coins we use. Write the amounts under each one.

 c   c   c   c   c   c

B Draw coins in each purse to make up the amount shown.
Use the **least** amount of coins possible.

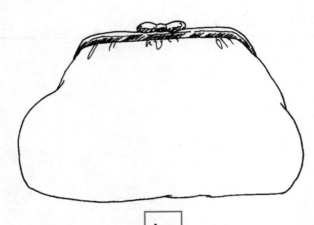

4c

8c

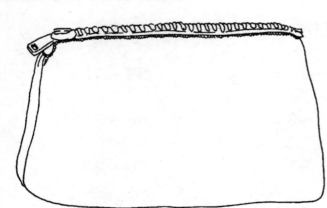

27c

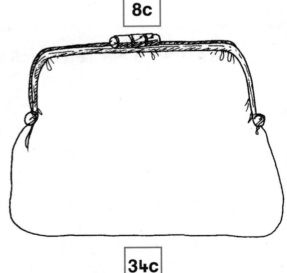

34c

C What 2 coins would you use to make up?

7c _____ ,   11c _____ ,   25c _____ ,   51c _____ ,

30c _____ ,   70c _____ ,   6c _____ ,   40c _____ .

A Draw coins in each money box to make up the amount shown. Use the least amount of coins possible.

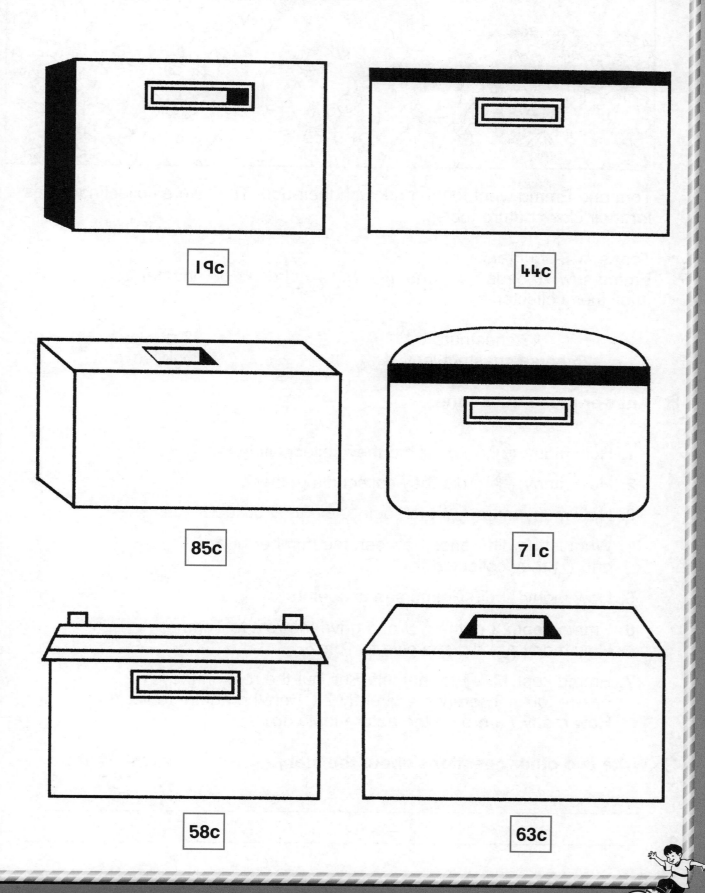

19c

44c

85c

71c

58c

63c

A **Read the story. Colour the picture.**

Tom and Emma went to the park with their dad. They were collecting things for their class nature tables.

Tom saw **8** squirrels .
Emma saw **13** birds on one tree and **16** birds on another tree.
In all they collected:

47 chestnuts   **32** acorns
25 horse-chestnut leaves   **13** oak leaves

B **Answer these questions.**

1. How many   and   did they collect altogether?

2. How many   did they collect altogether?

3. How many more   than oak   did they collect?

4. What is the difference between the number of   and   they collected?

5. How many   did Emma see altogether?

6. Emma kept **23** of the   and gave the rest to Tom. How many   did she give to Tom?

7. Emma kept **11**   for herself. She put the rest on the nature table. There were already **7**   on the nature table. How many   are on the nature table now?

C **Write two other questions about the story.**

_____

_____

Across

1. 24 + 21 = ☐
2. 59 − 23 = ☐
3. 14 + 13 = ☐
4. 32 + 26 = ☐
5. 73 − 41 = ☐
7. 56 − 14 = ☐
8. 27 − 14 = ☐
9. 89 − 30 = ☐
10. 41 + 47 = ☐
11. 67 + 10 = ☐

Down

1. 57 − 10 = ☐
2. 12 + 26 = ☐
3. 20 + 3 = ☐
4. 40 + 12 = ☐
5. 75 − 43 = ☐
6. 33 + 10 = ☐
7. 29 + 20 = ☐
8. 9 + 9 = ☐
9. 20 + 30 = ☐
10. 54 + 33 = ☐

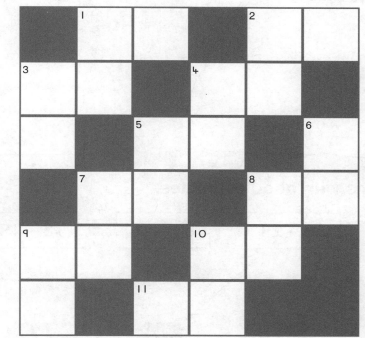

A Fill in the numbers in the boxes.

+	O	I	2
O			
I		2	
2			
3			
4			
5			

B Draw coins in each purse to make up the amount shown.

16c

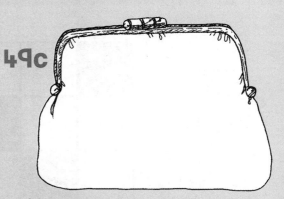

49c

C Match the sums with good estimates.

93 – 32	68 – 29	83 – 46	73 – 19	41 – 24

20	30	40	50	60

D Complete these symmetrical shapes.

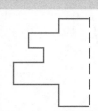

Tom has **2 tens** and **14 units**.
He wants to swap his **14 units** for a **ten**.
How many tens and units will he have when he makes the swap?

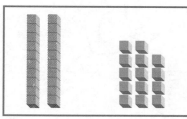 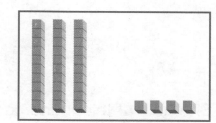

2 tens and 14 units = 3 tens and 4 units

A What swaps will Tom get for these tens and units?

1. 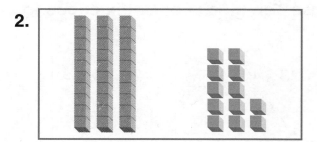 =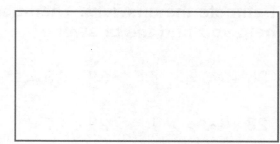

2. 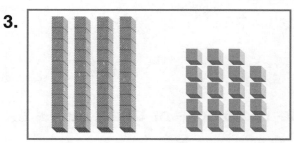 =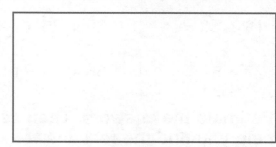

3. 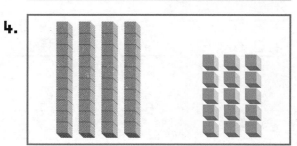 =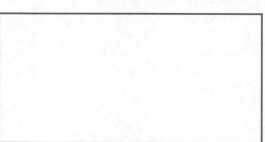

4. 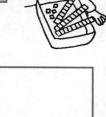 =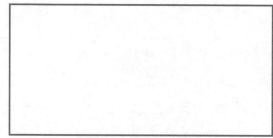

Jill has **36** telephone cards.
She finds **7** more.
How many telephone cards has she now?

$$36 + 7 = \boxed{43}$$

$$\begin{array}{r} 3\ 7 \\ +\ \ _1 6 \\ \hline 4\ 3 \end{array}$$

Answer: She has **43** telephone cards.

A **Try these. Use Base Ten blocks or Unifix cubes to help you.**

16 + 7 = ☐   24 + 9 = ☐   48 + 3 = ☐   36 + 6 = ☐

45 + 5 = ☐   26 + 8 = ☐   54 + 6 = ☐   67 + 7 = ☐

19 + 5 = ☐   78 + 6 = ☐   29 + 8 = ☐   44 + 7 = ☐

56 + 4 = ☐   28 + 9 = ☐   37 + 6 = ☐   46 + 8 = ☐

B **Estimate the answers. Then use Base Ten blocks or Unifix cubes to help you find the answer.**

35 + 36 = ☐   39 + 23 = ☐   38 + 49 = ☐   26 + 26 = ☐

28 + 48 = ☐   29 + 27 = ☐   47 + 36 = ☐   56 + 27 = ☐

19 + 36 = ☐   28 + 25 = ☐   33 + 39 = ☐   25 + 48 = ☐

27 + 54 = ☐   65 + 19 = ☐   23 + 47 = ☐   61 + 19 = ☐

C **Estimate the answers. Then use Base Ten blocks or Unifix cubes to help you find the real answer.**

$$\begin{array}{r} 2\ 3 \\ +\ 1\ 7 \\ \hline \end{array}$$
$$\begin{array}{r} 1\ 9 \\ +\ 1\ 2 \\ \hline \end{array}$$
$$\begin{array}{r} 3\ 4 \\ +\ 2\ 7 \\ \hline \end{array}$$
$$\begin{array}{r} 2\ 5 \\ +\ 3\ 6 \\ \hline \end{array}$$
$$\begin{array}{r} 2\ 9 \\ +\ 4\ 6 \\ \hline \end{array}$$
$$\begin{array}{r} 4\ 8 \\ +\ 2\ 7 \\ \hline \end{array}$$

$$\begin{array}{r} 3\ 6 \\ +\ 3\ 8 \\ \hline \end{array}$$
$$\begin{array}{r} 5\ 4 \\ +\ 2\ 7 \\ \hline \end{array}$$
$$\begin{array}{r} 6\ 3 \\ +\ 1\ 9 \\ \hline \end{array}$$
$$\begin{array}{r} 5\ 1 \\ +\ 2\ 9 \\ \hline \end{array}$$
$$\begin{array}{r} 6\ 2 \\ +\ 1\ 9 \\ \hline \end{array}$$
$$\begin{array}{r} 7\ 4 \\ +\ 1\ 9 \\ \hline \end{array}$$

Here are **3** different T-shirts.

Here are **3** different pairs of shorts.

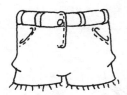  

A **How many different outfits can you make?**
Draw them in the box below. One is done.

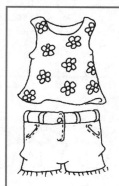

A What part (fraction) of each shape is coloured: $\frac{1}{2}$ or $\frac{1}{4}$?

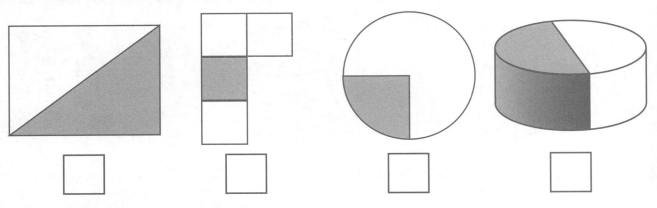

B Colour one **half** of each group.

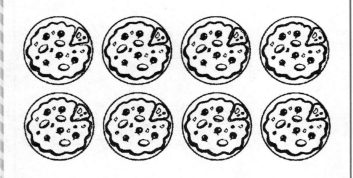

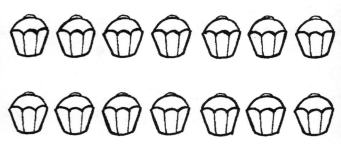

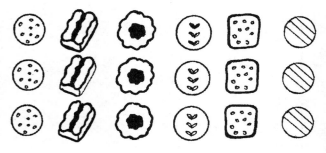

A There are **20** sweets in all. There are **5** sweets in **each quarter** ($\frac{1}{4}$).
Colour a **quarter** of the sweets.

$\frac{1}{4}$ of 20 is ☐ .

B Colour a **quarter** of the books.

$\frac{1}{4}$ of 8 is ☐ .

C

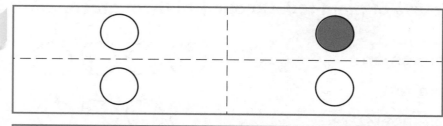

$\frac{1}{4}$ of 4 is ☐

$\frac{1}{4}$ of 16 = ☐

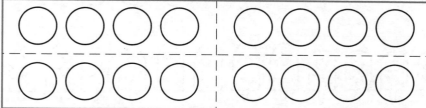

$\frac{1}{4}$ of ☐ = ☐

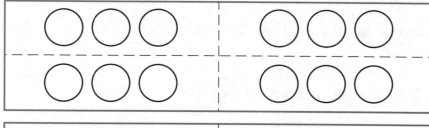

$\frac{1}{4}$ of ☐ = ☐

A Colour $\frac{1}{4}$ of these **blue.**   Colour $\frac{1}{2}$ of these **red.**

B Colour $\frac{1}{4}$ of these **green.**   Colour $\frac{1}{2}$ of these **brown.**

C Here are 8 apples. Colour $\frac{1}{2}$ of them **red.** Colour $\frac{1}{2}$ of them **green.**

1. How many apples are **green**?

2. How many apples are **red**?

3. How many apples are not **red**?

D

1. What fraction of the ice pops are orange-flavoured ?

2. How many ice pops are banana-flavoured ?

3. What fraction of the ice pops are lemon-flavoured ?

4. How many ice pops are apple-flavoured ?

THE CALENDAR

— April —

Sunday	Monday	Tuesday	Wednesday	Thursday	Friday	Saturday
						1
2	3	4	5	6	7	8
9	10	11	12	13	14	15
16	17	18	19	20	21	22
23	24	25	26	27	28	29
30						

A **Look at the calendar page. Write the day.**

April 11th _____   April 6th _____   April 19th _____

April 23rd _____   Two days after April 13th _____

B **Write each date.**

The second Monday	10th	4 days after April 17th	_____
The fourth Sunday	_____	1 week after April 3rd	_____
The third Wednesday	_____	2 weeks before April 15th	_____
The first Saturday	_____	2 weeks after April 3rd	_____
The third Friday	_____	5 days before April 12th	_____
The last Sunday	_____	3 weeks before April 30th	_____
3 days after April 16th	_____	1 week after April 1st	_____

C **To do at home. Use a calendar to find out:**

1. How many months and days it is until Christmas. _____

2. How many months and days it is until your birthday. _____

65

A Keep a diary for a week.

Monday: _____

_____

_____

Tuesday: _____

_____

_____

Wednesday: _____

_____

_____

Thursday: _____

_____

_____

Friday: _____

_____

_____

Saturday: _____

_____

_____

Sunday: _____

_____

_____

A Colour each **season** in a different colour.

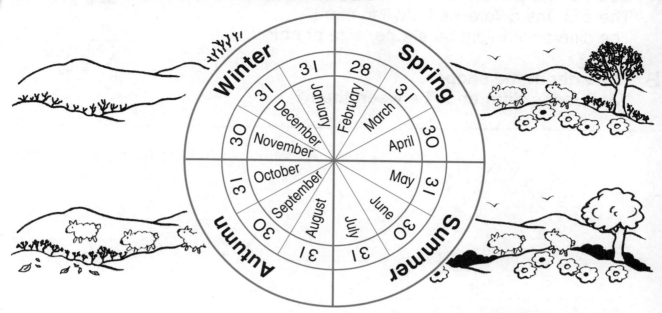

B Finish each sentence.

1. There are ☐ hours in a day.

2. There are ☐ months in a year.

I day = 24 hours
I week = 7 days
I year = 12 months

3. The 4th month of the year is _____.

4. The last month of the year is _____.

5. March is in the season of _____.

6. August is in the season of _____.

7. _____ is the last month of spring.

8. _____, _____, _____,

are the months of winter.

9. The months that have 30 days only are: _____,

_____, _____ and _____.

10. The shortest season is the season of _____.

11. Hallowe'en falls in the month of _____.

12. _____ is my favourite month because _____

_____.

C [P] **Make a bar graph of the favourite months in your class.**

A **Look at the pairs of 2-D shapes below.**
There is **one** difference between them.
The difference might be **shape**, **size** or **colour**.

B **Write about the shapes.**
What is the difference between them?

I.

One triangle is large.

2.

3.

4.

68

A Beside each shape, draw a shape that is different in **one way** from the one given.

1.

2.

3.

4.

Sally asked each pupil in her class, "What is your favourite fruit?".
She made a **pictogram** of the answers.

Strawberries	🍓 🍓 🍓 🍓 🍓 🍓
Pears	🍐 🍐
Bananas	🍌 🍌 🍌 🍌 🍌 🍌 🍌
Oranges	🍊 🍊 🍊 🍊
Apples	🍎 🍎 🍎 🍎 🍎 🍎 🍎 🍎 🍎 🍎

A **Look at the pictogram and answer the questions.**

1. What is the favourite fruit? _____

2. What fruit is liked least? _____

3. How many more children liked strawberries than pears? _____

4. How many more children liked apples than bananas? _____

5. How many children answered Sally's question? _____

B **Here is another way to show the story:**
The boxes are coloured for pupils who liked apples best.
Colour the boxes for pupils who gave other answers.

Strawberries										
Pears										
Bananas										
Oranges										
Apples										

A **Try these sums.**

1.
```
   2 4        6 3        3 7        2 8        4 2        5 0
 + 1 3      +   7      + 2 0      + 1 9      + 2 5      + 3 9
```

2.
```
   2 9        2 3        2 0        3 9        2 8        7 1
 + 1 5      + 4 6      + 5 4      + 3 9      + 4 6      + 1 9
```

B 20 children got new pencils. $\frac{1}{2}$ of the children got a blue pencil. $\frac{1}{4}$ of the children got a red pencil. $\frac{1}{4}$ of the children got a yellow pencil.
Colour the pencils.

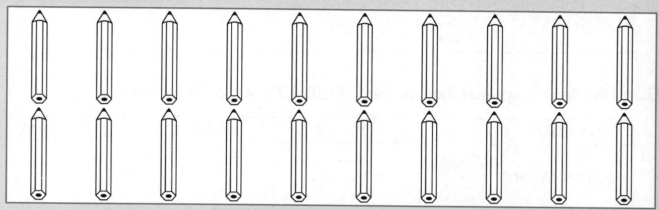

1. How many children got a **blue** pencil? ☐

2. How many children got a **red** pencil? ☐

C **Fill in the dates and days that are missing from this calendar.**

— October —						
Sunday	M _ _ _ _ _	T _ _ _ _ _ _	Wednesday	T _ _ _ _ _ _ _	F _ _ _ _ _	Saturday
1				5		
	9					14
			18	19		
22					27	
29						

A Use different objects to cover your table top. How many of each one are needed? (Don't forget to make an estimate first.)

To Cover My Table		
Object	**Estimate**	**Amount**
Envelopes		
Playing cards		
Copies		
Workbooks		

B In the last 4 spaces below, find items of your own to cover.

To cover	**Object**	**Estimate**	**Amount**
Maths Book			

C With your friend, find out which surface is greater; the top of your table or the top of your teacher's table.
Hint: Use playing cards, envelopes or copies.

A Colour the shape with the greatest area.
Colour the shape with the smallest area.
Which two shapes have about the same area?

1.

2.

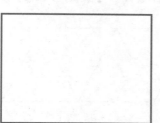

3.

4.

5.

6.

A **Colour:**

Green: an area of 3 △s.　　　　Red: an area of 4 △s.

Yellow: an area of 5 △s.　　　　Blue: an area of 6 △s.

B **How many △s are not shaded?** ☐

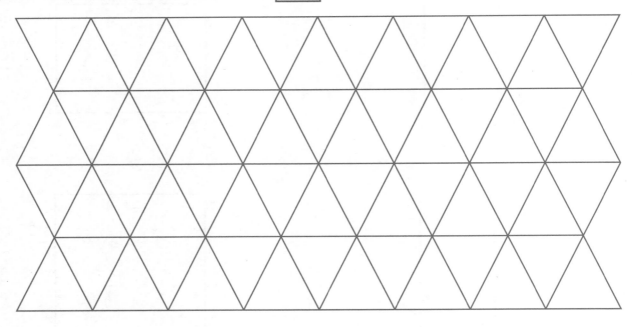

C **Use this squared paper to make shapes which cover 6 squares. One has been done for you. How many more can you find?**

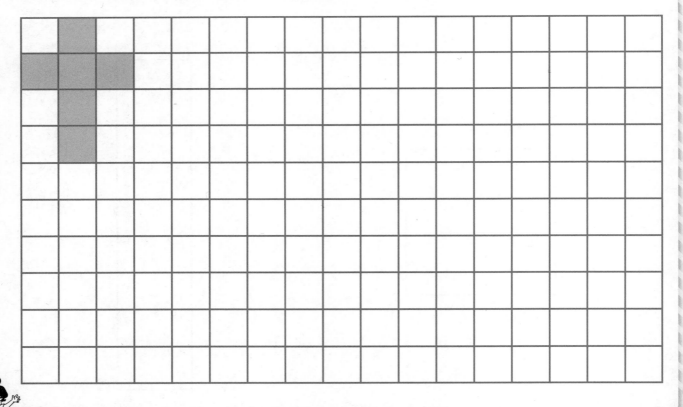

A Complete.

1.

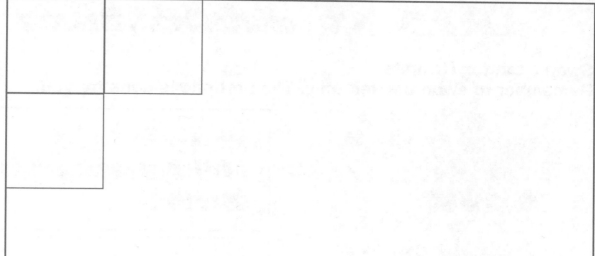

2.

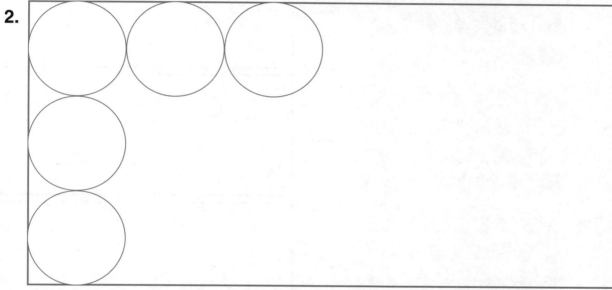

3.

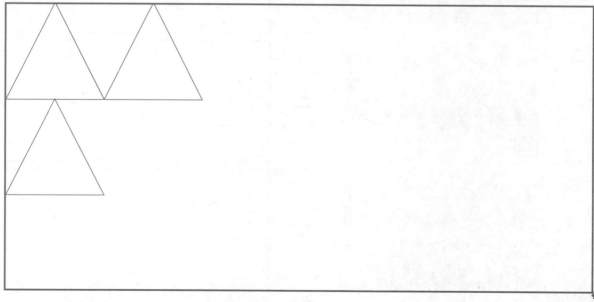

A **ten** can be swapped for **10 units** like this.

A Swap a **ten** for **10 units**.
Remember to swap **one ten** only. The first one is done for you.

1.  =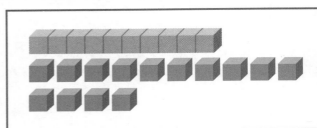

2. 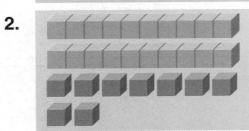 =

3. 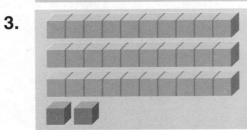 =

4. 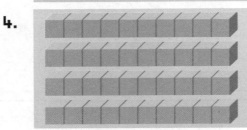 =

5. 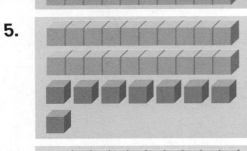 =

6. 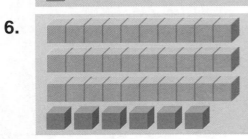 =

Tom has **31** sweets.
He gives **19** away.
How many has he left?

31 − 19 = ☐ **12**

```
  3 1
− 1 9
─────
  1 2
```

A **Use Base Ten blocks or Unifix cubes to do these.**

24 − 6 = ☐   27 − 9 = ☐   26 − 8 = ☐   21 − 9 = ☐

21 − 6 = ☐   23 − 9 = ☐   25 − 8 = ☐   22 − 4 = ☐

34 − 9 = ☐   33 − 5 = ☐   36 − 8 = ☐   35 − 6 = ☐

42 − 5 = ☐   46 − 9 = ☐   44 − 8 = ☐   51 − 7 = ☐

B **Use Base Ten blocks or Unifix cubes to do these.**

35 − 26 = ☐   50 − 29 = ☐   72 − 38 = ☐   46 − 27 = ☐

53 − 35 = ☐   50 − 19 = ☐   56 − 17 = ☐   84 − 39 = ☐

C **Use Base Ten blocks or Unifix cubes to do these.**

```
  3 8          4 2          5 5          4 1
− 1 9        − 1 6        − 1 8        − 1 5
```

```
  3 3          3 6          4 0          6 1
− 2 4        − 2 7        − 2 2        − 3 8
```

```
  4 5          6 6          7 3          5 2
− 2 9        − 3 9        − 2 8        − 3 5
```

```
  7 0          5 4          8 7          9 1
− 3 6        − 2 8        − 3 9        − 4 3
```

A **Find the letters and colour them in.**

Which letter is?

above **E** ☐

to the right of **B** ☐

below **F** ☐

to the left of **B** ☐

to the left of **E** ☐

below **E** ☐

below and to the left of **E** ☐

above and to the right of **H** ☐

to the right of **D** and to the left of **F** ☐

A	B	C
D	E	F
G	H	I

B **Fill in the boxes and find the word.**

O is above **U**

R is below **U**

S is to the right of **R**

T is above **S**

P is to the left of **U**

C is above **P**

M is above and to the right of **U**

E is below and to the left of **U**

	U	

C **Write the word you find here.** _____

A **Colour these objects that can tell you the time.**

egg-timer

candle-clock

water-clock

B **Try these.**

1. How many jumps can you do in a turn of an egg-timer?

_____

2. How many times can you bounce a ball in a turn of an egg-timer?

_____

3. How many times do you turn the egg-timer while your friend runs around the playground? _____

4. How much time passes between roll-call and break-time? Use a water-clock or a candle-clock. _____

C **Design your own clock faces. One is done for you.**

TIME

A What time does each clock show?

[ ] o'clock   [ ] o'clock   [ ] o'clock   [ ] o'clock

½ past [ ]   ½ past [ ]   ½ past [ ]   ½ past [ ]

B

When the **long hand** is pointing at **3** it is a **quarter past**.

When the **long hand** is pointing at **9** it is a **quarter to**.

What **fraction** of each clock is shaded? [ ]

C What time does each clock show?

¼ past [ ]   ¼ past [ ]   ¼ to [ ]   ¼ to [ ]

80

A **What time does each clock show?**

¼ past ☐   ¼ past ☐   ¼ to ☐   ¼ past ☐

___ to ___ ☐   ___ ___ ☐   ___ ___ ☐   ___ ___ ☐

B **Make your own clock face.**

You will need:

- a paper plate
- a paper fastener
- coloured card for hands
- colouring markers

C **P** **Show these times on your clock or on a clock-sheet.**

½ past 12	¼ past 8	¼ to 2
¼ to 11	¼ past 10	½ past 5
¼ to 7	¼ past 1	½ past 3
getting-up time	break-time	your favourite time

A Draw the times that are 2 hours later than the above times.

B Set the starting or finishing times on the ovens.

Dish	Cooking Time	Starting Time	Finishing Time
Reheat Pizza	$\frac{1}{4}$ hour		
Meat Pie	2 hours		
Muffins	$\frac{1}{2}$ hour		
Roast Chicken	3 hours		
Gingerbread	I hour		
Carrots	$\frac{1}{2}$ hour		

I hour = 6O minutes

½ hour = 3O minutes

Digital time is shown **below** each of these clocks.

| 4 : OO | II : OO | 2 : 3O |

A **P** Show these digital times on your own clock or on a clock-sheet.

| 2 : OO | 9 : OO | I : 3O | IO : OO | 3 : 3O |
| 4 : 3O | 7 : 3O | 6 : OO | 8 : 3O | 5 : OO |

B Match each time to a clue.

1.   9 : OO   Half way between 7 o'clock and 8 o'clock.

2.      One hour before IO o'clock.

3.   7 : 3O   ½ hour before 4 o'clock.

4.   [clock]   3 hours after ½ past 9.

5.   12 : 3O   After ½ past four but before 6 o'clock.

A **Look at this television guide. Answer the questions below.**

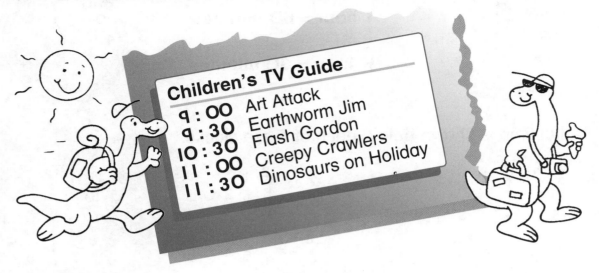

Children's TV Guide

9 : 00 Art Attack
9 : 30 Earthworm Jim
10 : 30 Flash Gordon
11 : 00 Creepy Crawlers
11 : 30 Dinosaurs on Holiday

1. At what time does *Art Attack* start? _____

2. What programme starts at ½ past ten? _____

3. What programme starts two hours later than *Art Attack*?
   _____

4. If you watched *Earthworm Jim* and *Flash Gordon*,
   how long would you spend watching television? _____

5. If *Dinosaurs on Holiday* is half an hour long,
   at what time will the next programme start? _____

6. Invent a name for the next programme. _____

B **Write your own time-table.**

Children's TV Guide

C **To do at home.**
Look at a television guide. Write the names of three programmes that start on the hour (an 'o'clock time') and three programmes that start at ½ past the hour.

A Finish the picture.

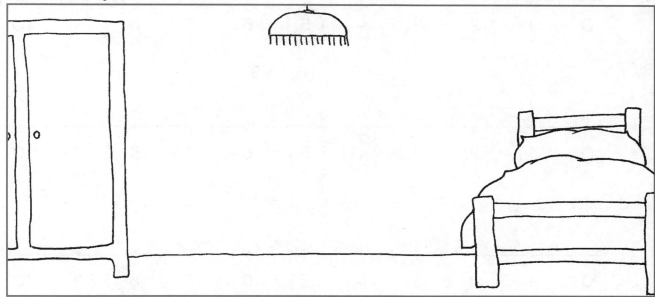

1. Draw a small 🗄 to the **left** of the bed.

2. Draw a 🛋 **between** the wardrobe and the small 🗄 .

3. Draw a 💻 on the **left** of the table.

4. Draw a 🕐 **on top** of the small 🗄 .

5. Draw 👞 **underneath** the bed.

6. Draw a 🖼 on the wall **above** the bed.

7. Draw a 👕 on the **bottom left corner** of the bed.

8. Draw a 🚗 on the **top right corner** of the bed.

B Find the hidden treasure. Give directions to your friend.

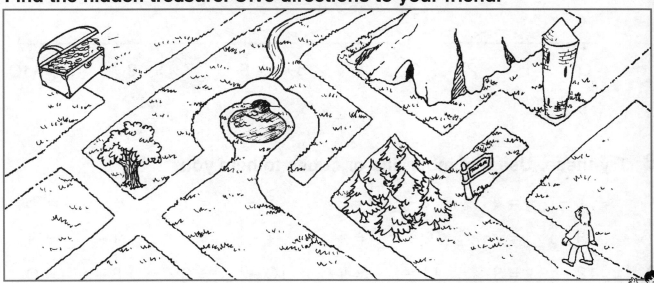

A

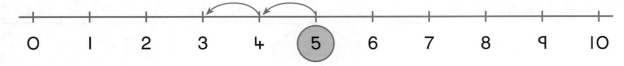

$$5 - \boxed{} = 3$$

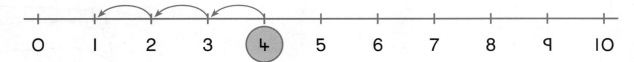

$$4 - \boxed{} = 1$$

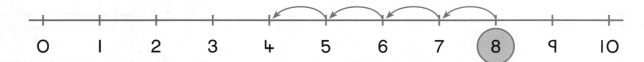

$$8 - \boxed{} = 4$$

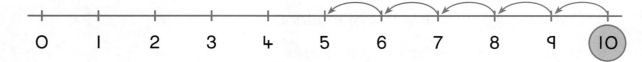

$$10 - \boxed{} = 5$$

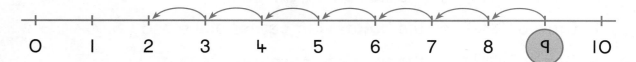

$$9 - \boxed{} = 2$$

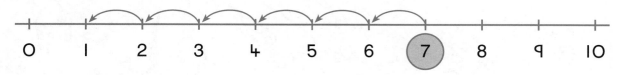

$$7 - \boxed{} = 1$$

B Try these. Use a number line or cubes to help you.

$7 - \boxed{} = 3$	$6 - \boxed{} = 2$	$5 - \boxed{} = 1$	$8 - \boxed{} = 5$
$9 - \boxed{} = 7$	$10 - \boxed{} = 4$	$4 - \boxed{} = 1$	$9 - \boxed{} = 4$
$12 - \boxed{} = 9$	$11 - \boxed{} = 4$	$10 - \boxed{} = 3$	$8 - \boxed{} = 0$

A Can you make pairs? Are there any left over? Use different colours.

1.

5.

2.

6.

3.

7.

4.

8.

4 is an **even** number.   7 is an **odd** number.

A List 10 **even** numbers.   2 __ __ __ __ __ __ __ __ __

List 10 **odd** numbers.   1 __ __ __ __ __ __ __ __ __

B Write **even** or **odd** beside each number.

4 ___even___   7 _____   10 _____   13 _____

8 _____   16 _____   17 _____   1 _____

21 _____   9 _____   12 _____   20 _____

27 _____   22 _____   30 _____   25 _____

29 _____   40 _____   2 _____   11 _____

C On this number-chart, colour all the **even** numbers, blue.

Colour all the **odd** numbers, red.

Can you find a pattern?

1	2	3	4	5	6	7	8	9	10
11	12	13	14	15	16	17	18	19	20
21	22	23	24	25	26	27	28	29	30
31	32	33	34	35	36	37	38	39	40
41	42	43	44	45	46	47	48	49	50
51	52	53	54	55	56	57	58	59	60

D Finish each number pattern.

1. 1   3   5   ____ ____ ____ ____

2. 4   6   8   ____ ____ ____ ____

3. 10   12   14   ____ ____ ____ ____

4. 25   27   29   ____ ____ ____ ____

5. 30   32   34   ____ ____ ____ ____

6. 11   13   15   ____ ____ ____ ____

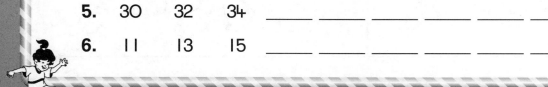

88

A

1. Add these numbers.

$2 + 7 + 8 =$ ☐ $3 + 5 + 3 =$ ☐ $4 + 4 + 6 =$ ☐

How did you find the answers?

2. Look for pairs that add up to 10.

$4 + 8 + 6 =$ ☐ $(4 + 6) + 8 =$ ☐ $10 + 8 =$ ☐

3. Look for doubles.

$7 + 5 + 7 =$ ☐ $(7 + 7) + 5 =$ ☐ $14 + 5 =$ ☐

B **Add these numbers. Look for an easy way to find the answers.**

$1 + 7 + 9 =$ ☐ $9 + 1 + 6 =$ ☐ $8 + 4 + 6 =$ ☐ $8 + 5 + 2 =$ ☐

$7 + 8 + 3 =$ ☐ $5 + 5 + 3 =$ ☐ $9 + 6 + 1 =$ ☐ $1 + 8 + 9 =$ ☐

C $4 + 7 + 4 =$ ☐ $3 + 8 + 3 =$ ☐ $7 + 6 + 6 =$ ☐ $5 + 5 + 1 =$ ☐

$5 + 6 + 6 =$ ☐ $2 + 2 + 9 =$ ☐ $7 + 2 + 7 =$ ☐ $7 + 4 + 7 =$ ☐

D

3	1	6	6	4	8	10	7
6	4	2	7	8	2	9	7
+ 7	+ 9	+ 6	+ 4	+ 4	+ 5	+ 0	+ 2

☐ ☐ ☐ ☐ ☐ ☐ ☐ ☐

E

1.

| 3 9 | 4 1 | 3 8 | 2 5 | 5 0 | 3 8 |
| + 1 6 | + 2 8 | + 3 6 | + 1 9 | + 2 5 | + 4 2 |

2.

| 6 0 | 5 2 | 2 7 | 2 9 | 4 9 | 5 3 |
| + 2 6 | + 2 3 | + 2 7 | + 1 6 | + 1 1 | + 1 4 |

3.

| 2 8 | 1 7 | 5 3 | 3 7 | 6 0 | 8 4 |
| + 6 0 | + 5 4 | + 4 1 | + 4 8 | + 3 6 | + 1 3 |

Frank's class kept a record of the weather for the month of March. They made a pictogram of their findings.

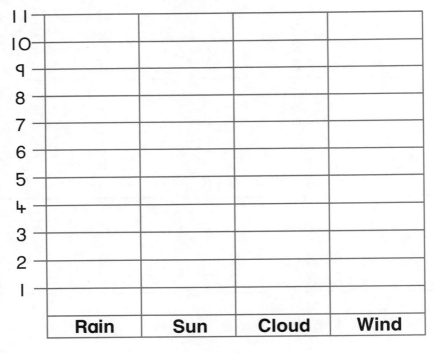

A Show what they found on this block graph.
Remember to colour a box for each day.

B To talk about.
What story does this graph tell you?

A

bucket

jug

bottle

carton

The _____ holds the **most** liquid. The _____ holds the **least** liquid.

B **Estimate** how many cartons will fill each container with water.
Then find the **actual** number of cartons.

Container	Estimate	Number of cartons

C Write the containers in order from **least** capacity to **greatest** capacity.

1. carton _____ 2. _____ 3. _____ 4. _____

D Design your own
containers for holding
these liquids:
tea; lemonade; water;
chocolate milkshake.

A Tick (✓) the objects you would use to fill these containers,

B **To do at home.**
Find containers that hold about **1** litre.

A Find containers that measure more than 1 litre, about 1 litre, ½ litre and ¼ litre. Draw pictures of them in the correct boxes

About 1 litre	More than 1 litre
About ½ litre	About ¼ litre

B Find out how much each of the following containers hold.

	Jug	Bottle	Carton	Cup	Can
About ¼ litre					
About ½ litre					
About 1 litre					
More than 1 litre					

C Use ¼ litre, ½ litre and 1 litre containers to answer these questions.

1. How many ½ litres of water fill the 1 litre container? _____

2. How many ¼ litres fill the 1 litre container? _____

3. How many ¼ litres fill the ½ litre container? _____

A Colour in all the **even** numbers. You should find a small word.

15	6	33	32	8	30
7	28	9	49	14	1
23	12	17	35	46	29
41	44	21	13	28	47

B Try these.

```
   3 6        4 3        5 4        3 5        9 3        7 6
 - 2 4      - 1 7      - 2 0      -   8      - 2 1      - 4 7


   8 4        4 1        3 7        5 5        9 0        4 3
 - 2 9      -   9      - 2 1      - 1 6      - 1 6      - 2 9


   7 3        7 0        5 1        4 0        6 4        3 8
 - 3 3      - 2 8      - 1 9      - 1 8      - 4 7      - 2 0
```

C What time will it be half an hour later than these times?

½ past ☐   _____   _____   _____

D Write the new clock times in **digital time**.

☐ : ☐	☐ : ☐	☐ : ☐	☐ : ☐

A Put these flags into groups of 10.
How many groups are there?

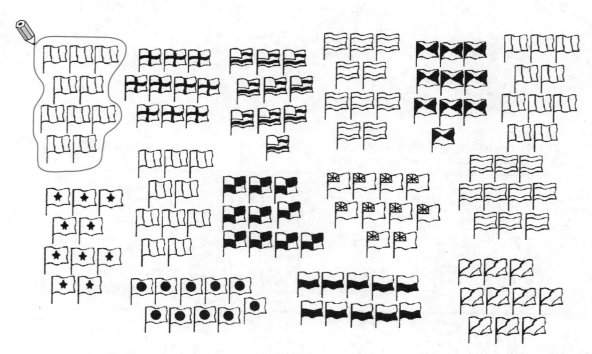

B Put these cars into groups of 10. How many groups are there?
How many cars are left over?

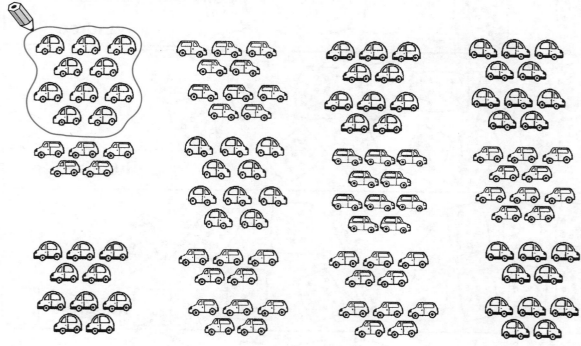

C To do.
You need a small jar filled with counters. Each pupil makes an estimate of the number of counters in the jar. Count them by putting them in groups of ten. Whose estimate was closest to the real amount?

A **Ring 10 bags of sweets in each row. Write the numbers.**

| 10 tens **make** 1 hundred. | ☐ hundred | **0** tens |

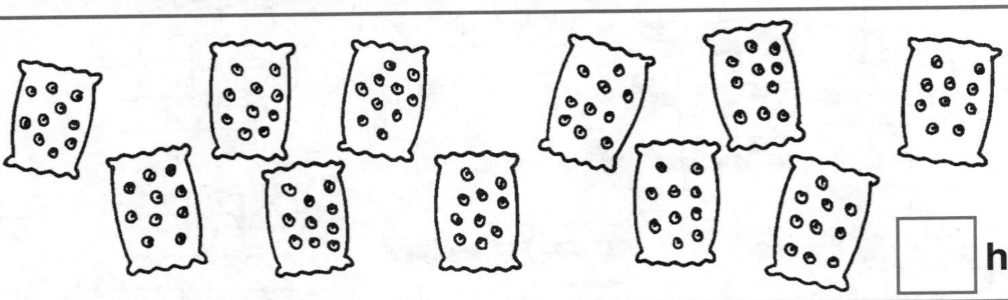

☐ hundred ☐ ten

☐ hundred ☐ tens

☐ hundred ☐ tens

☐ hundred ☐ tens

☐ hundred ☐ tens

A Colour 10 bags of sweets in each row. Write the numbers.

[ ] hundred [ ] tens [ ] units

[ ] hundred [ ] tens [ ] units

[ ] hundred [ ] tens [ ] units

[ ] hundred [ ] tens [ ] units

[ ] hundred [ ] tens [ ] unit

[ ] hundred [ ] tens [ ] units

10 **tens** can be swapped for one **hundred** like this:

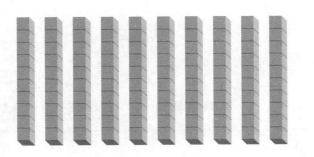

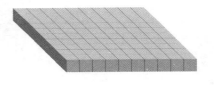

| One hundred   100 |

A How many **units** can be swapped for one **hundred**?

B Write the number shown by the Base Ten blocks.

Hundreds	Tens	Units	Number
			_____
			_____
			_____
			_____
			_____

A **Write the number shown by the Base Ten blocks.**

Hundreds	Tens	Units	Number
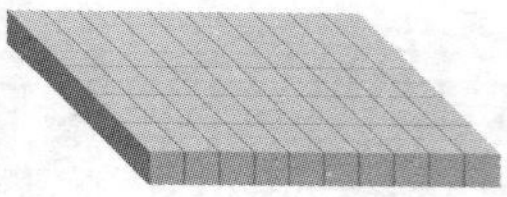	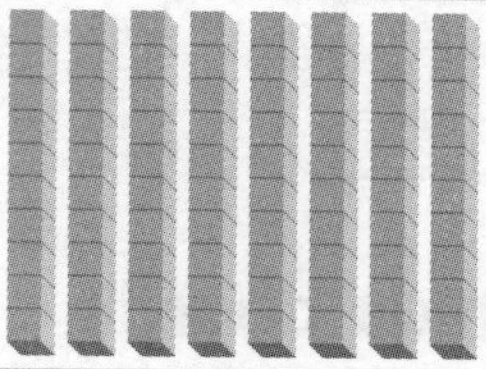		_____
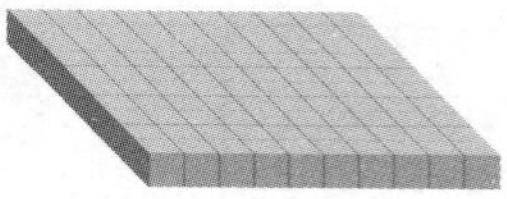	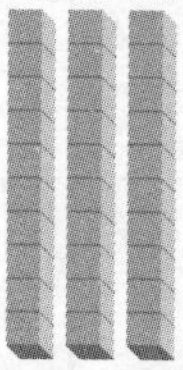	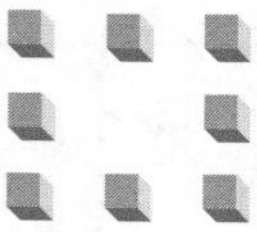	_____
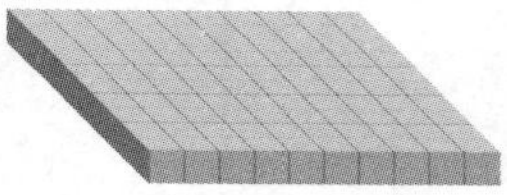	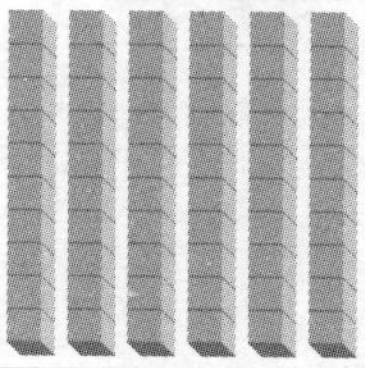		_____
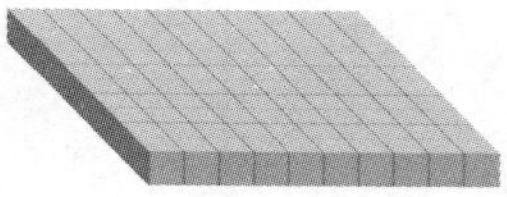			_____
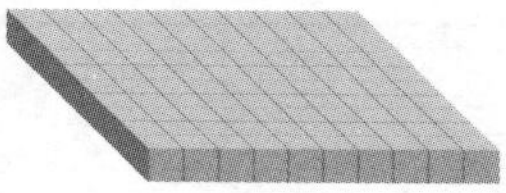		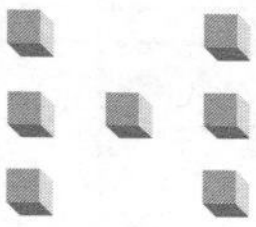	_____
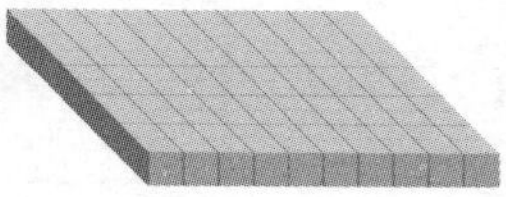	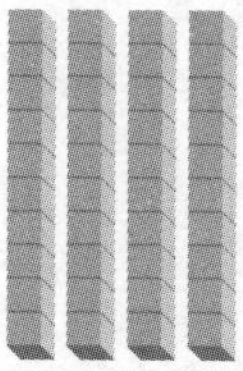		_____
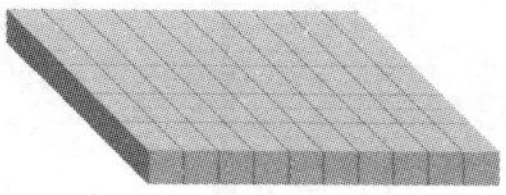		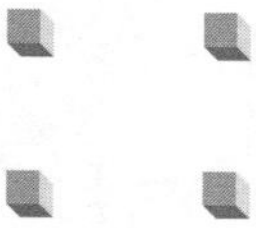	_____
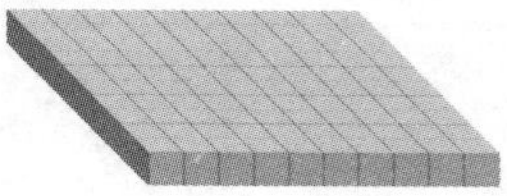			_____

B **Use Base Ten blocks to show these numbers.**

124   138   151   190   102   115

A Count in tens.

10 , 20 , _____ , _____ , _____ ,

_____ , _____ , _____ , _____ , _____ .

B Draw these numbers on the place-value boards using Base Ten blocks.

128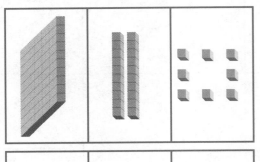

134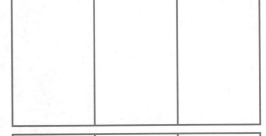

145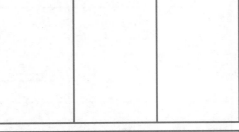

157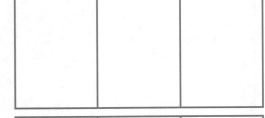

181

162

173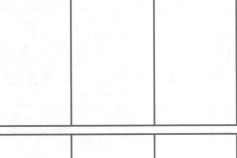

126

191

154

A **Draw these numbers on the place-value boards using Base Ten blocks.**

179

180

144

114

130

103

119

106

111

160

110

150

A Write the number that comes after:

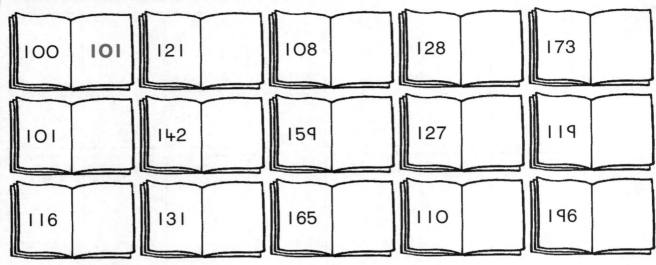

100	**101**	121		108		128		173	
101		142		159		127		119	
116		131		165		110		196	

B Write the number that comes before:

	103	104		126		154		111		101
	178		187		139		190		143
	131		170		127		174		156

C Write the number that comes between:

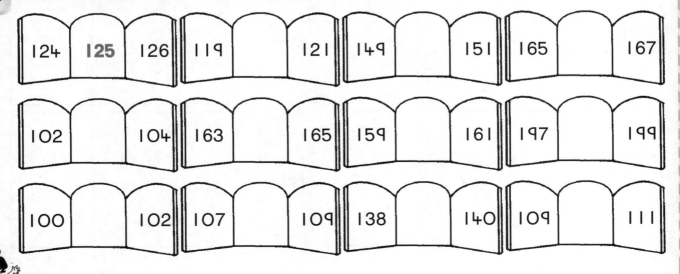

124	**125**	126	119		121	149		151	165		167
102		104	163		165	159		161	197		199
100		102	107		109	138		140	109		111

102

A **Write the numbers that are missing from the boxes.**

1.

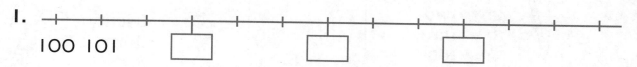

100 101

2.

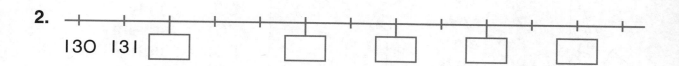

130 131

3.

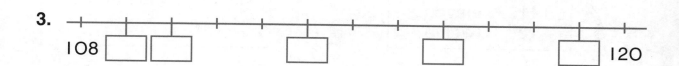

108   120

4.

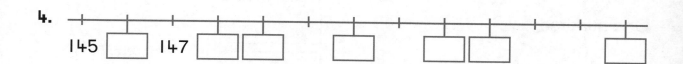

145   147

5.

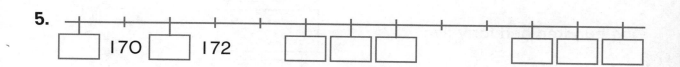

170   172

6.

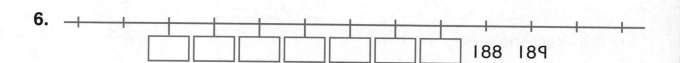

188 189

7.

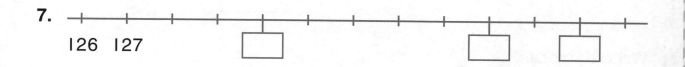

126 127

8.

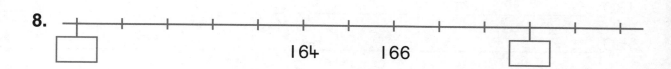

164   166

9.

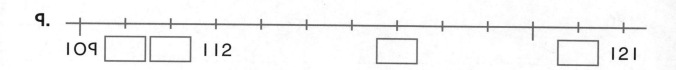

109   112   121

NUMBERS IN WORDS

1:	one
2:	two
3:	three
4:	four
5:	five
6:	six
7:	seven
8:	eight
9:	nine
10:	ten
11:	eleven
12:	twelve

20:	twenty
30:	thirty
40:	forty
50:	fifty
60:	sixty
70:	seventy
80:	eighty
90:	ninety
100:	one hundred

A **Write in numbers.**

One hundred

One hundred and twenty four

One hundred and forty five

One hundred and sixty

One hundred and ninety

One hundred and eight

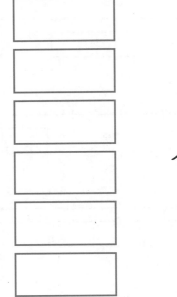

B **Write in words.**

130 _____

150 _____

184 _____

196 _____

111 _____

107 _____

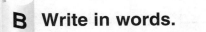

A **Help Pirate Pam find the treasure.**
Colour the path she has to take. She cannot go through a **green** square. Finish writing the directions.

Right
Left
Up
Down

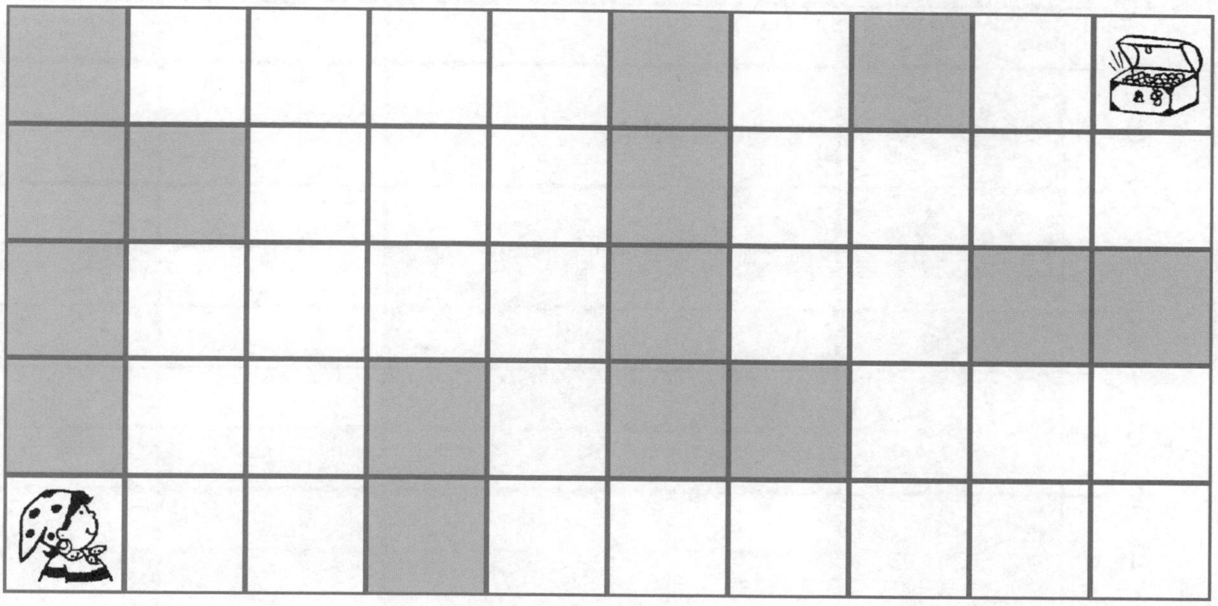

I. <u>Walk 2 squares to the right.</u>

2. _____

3. _____

4. _____

5. _____

6. _____

7. _____

8. _____

B **Pick one of these boxes but don't say which one you picked!**
Give your friend directions for finding it. Can they reach the right box?

A block graph of breakfast cereals eaten by a class.

	12				
11					
10					
9					
8					
7					
6					
5					
4					
3					
2					
1					

Cornflakes   Wheat Pops   Muesli   Frost Bites   Porridge

A **Answer these questions.**

1. How many pupils had Wheat Pops for breakfast? _____

2. How many pupils had Muesli for breakfast? _____

3. How many **more** pupils had Cornflakes than Frost Bites? _____

4. How many **fewer** pupils had Porridge than Cornflakes? _____

5. How many pupils altogether had Cornflakes, Wheat Pops and Porridge? _____

6. How many pupils are in this class? _____

7. What is your favourite breakfast cereal? _____

B **To do.**
Make a graph of the favourite cereals in your class.
Write the names of some healthy breakfast cereals.

A **How many are there?**

1.

   4   +   ___   +   ___

2.

   ___   +   ___   +   ___   +   ___

3.

   ___   +   ___   +   ___   +   ___

4.
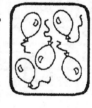  

   ___   +   ___   +   ___

5.

   ___   +   ___   +   ___

B **Use the number line to help you do these:**

0 1 2 3 4 5 6 7 8 9 10 11 12 13 14 15 16 17 18 19 20

Count in 2s as far as 20.   Count in 3s as far as 18.
Count in 4s as far as 20.   Count in 5s as far as 20.

C **Can you count in 10s as far as 100?**

A

Start at 2.
Colour every 2nd number, green.

Can you see a pattern?

Finish this pattern:

2, 4, _____, _____, _____, _____,

_____, _____, _____, 20.

1	2	3	4	5	6	7	8	9	10
11	12	13	14	15	16	17	18	19	20
21	22	23	24	25	26	27	28	29	30
31	32	33	34	35	36	37	38	39	40
41	42	43	44	45	46	47	48	49	50
51	52	53	54	55	56	57	58	59	60
61	62	63	64	65	66	67	68	69	70
71	72	73	74	75	76	77	78	79	80
81	82	83	84	85	86	87	88	89	90
91	92	93	94	95	96	97	98	99	100

B

Start at 3.
Colour every 3rd number, blue.

Can you see a pattern?

Finish this pattern:

3, 6, _____, _____, _____, _____,

_____, _____, _____, 30.

1	2	3	4	5	6	7	8	9	10
11	12	13	14	15	16	17	18	19	20
21	22	23	24	25	26	27	28	29	30
31	32	33	34	35	36	37	38	39	40
41	42	43	44	45	46	47	48	49	50
51	52	53	54	55	56	57	58	59	60
61	62	63	64	65	66	67	68	69	70
71	72	73	74	75	76	77	78	79	80
81	82	83	84	85	86	87	88	89	90
91	92	93	94	95	96	97	98	99	100

C

Start at 4.
Colour every 4th number, red.

Can you see a pattern?

Finish this pattern:

4, 8, _____, _____, _____, _____,

_____, _____, _____, 40.

1	2	3	4	5	6	7	8	9	10
11	12	13	14	15	16	17	18	19	20
21	22	23	24	25	26	27	28	29	30
31	32	33	34	35	36	37	38	39	40
41	42	43	44	45	46	47	48	49	50
51	52	53	54	55	56	57	58	59	60
61	62	63	64	65	66	67	68	69	70
71	72	73	74	75	76	77	78	79	80
81	82	83	84	85	86	87	88	89	90
91	92	93	94	95	96	97	98	99	100

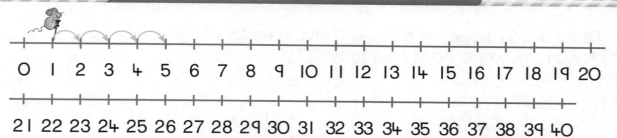

O 1 2 3 4 5 6 7 8 9 10 11 12 13 14 15 16 17 18 19 20

21 22 23 24 25 26 27 28 29 30 31 32 33 34 35 36 37 38 39 40

A What number is 4 jumps after 1? ☐   What number is 2 jumps after 9? ☐

What number is 6 jumps after 15? ☐   What number is 4 jumps after 28? ☐

B Mouse starts at number 14 and takes jumps of 1.
Write his first 10 landing spots.

⑭ 15 16

C Write his landing spots on this number line.

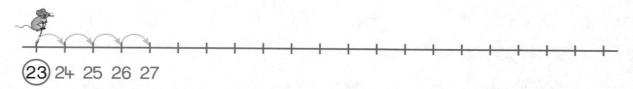

㉓ 24 25 26 27

D He takes jumps of 2. Write his first 10 landing spots.

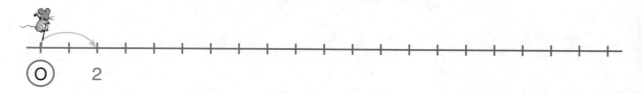

⓪   2

E Molly takes jumps of 2. Write her first 10 landing spots.

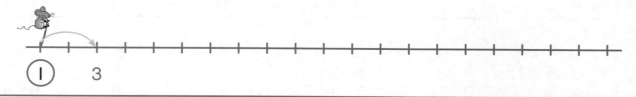

① 3

F Mum takes jumps of 5. Write her landing spots.

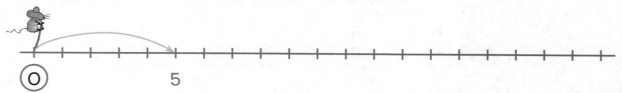

⓪   5

There are **51** pages in a book. I have read **26** of them.
How many pages have I left to read?

51 – 26 = ⬜

```
  5 1
– 2 6
─────
```

A **Try these. Be careful! Not all of them need a swap.**

48 – 16 = ⬜   39 – 19 = ⬜   53 – 27 = ⬜

81 – 50 = ⬜   30 – 27 = ⬜   91 – 58 = ⬜

39 – 20 = ⬜   65 – 37 = ⬜   74 – 59 = ⬜

81 – 59 = ⬜   78 – 69 = ⬜   45 – 17 = ⬜

B

```
  3 4       4 1       2 9       7 2       7 1       6 8
– 1 7     –   8     – 1 2     – 3 7     – 2 0     – 4 2
─────     ─────     ─────     ─────     ─────     ─────
```

```
  6 0       5 2       8 7       3 3       4 6       4 9
– 2 6     – 2 3     – 3 7     – 1 6     – 2 3     – 1 9
─────     ─────     ─────     ─────     ─────     ─────
```

```
  8 4       9 2       6 3       2 8       3 5       7 7
– 2 1     – 3 5     – 5 1     – 1 9     – 1 6     – 5 9
─────     ─────     ─────     ─────     ─────     ─────
```

```
  5 8       8 6       9 3       8 8       4 9       6 0
– 4 9     – 7 9     – 6 4     – 6 6     – 2 9     – 2 9
─────     ─────     ─────     ─────     ─────     ─────
```

Long ago, people measured distances in:

paces

spans

cubits

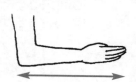

A **Measure around the classroom using paces, spans, cubits.**
Don't forget to estimate first.

Object		Measured with	Estimate	Amount
Height of chair		Spans		
Width of chair		Cubits		
Length of table		Spans		
Width of table		Cubits		
Height of table		Spans		
Length of blackboard	4 + 14 = 35 ✓	Cubits		
Short side of classroom		Paces		
Long side of classroom		Spans		
Length of bookshelf		Spans		
Width of bookshelf		Cubits		
Width of door		Spans		

B **Did everyone in your class get the same answer?**
Why might some of the answers be different?

C **To do at home.**
Measure objects at home using spans, paces and cubits.

We can measure length using different objects, for example:

lollipop sticks    links    pencils

A **Can you think of other objects you could use for measuring length?**

B **To do.**
Measure objects using lollipop sticks, links or pencils.
Don't forget to estimate first.

Object		Measured with	Estimate	Amount
The side of a cover				
The side of a chair				
The side of a table				
One of your shoes				
One of your sleeves				
Your school bag				
A bookshelf				
A door				
Your own choice of object				

C **To do in class.**
1. Measure your height using links.
2. Measure from finger tip to finger tip using links. (Stretch out your arms.)
3. Measure around your head using links.
4. Talk about what you find.
5. Make a graph of the heights in your class. Use links.

A Why is it not always a good idea to use units like pencils, spans or paces for measuring length?

> We can use the metre to measure length.

B Find objects in your classroom that measure:

about 1 metre   less than 1 metre   more than 1 metre

Write or draw them in this circle.

Less than 1 metre

About 1 metre

More than 1 metre

A Use metre-strips and half-metre strips to measure around the classroom.

Object		Estimate	Amount
Length of bookshelf			
Width of door			
Height of chair			
Height of table			
Length of room			
Width of room			
Width of window-ledge			
Length of blackboard	4 + 14 = 35 ✓		
Your own height			

B Write **more than** or **less than** for each sentence.

1. A lunchbox measures _____ _____ a metre.

2. A car measures _____ _____ a metre.

3. A man measures _____ _____ a metre.

4. A goldfish measures _____ _____ a metre.

5. A pencil measures _____ _____ a metre.

6. A schoolbag measures _____ _____ a metre.

7. A lorry measures _____ _____ a metre.

A Is it a good idea to use a metre-strip to measure objects like:
a pencil? an eraser? a milk-carton?

We can use a **centimetre** to measure the length of short objects.

> ### 100 centimetres = 1 metre

Objects that measure about 1 centimetre.

B Make a list of 6 objects in the classroom that measure about
1 centimetre.

1. _____   2. _____   3. _____

4. _____   5. _____   6. _____

This measures about
10 centimetres.

C Make a list of 6 objects in the classroom that measure about
10 centimetres.

1. _____   2. _____   3. _____

4. _____   5. _____   6. _____

D Measure these lines using your ruler or a 10 centimetre strip.

A =

B =

C =

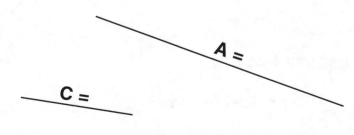

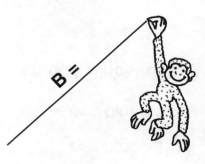

D =

E =

A How could you measure the length of this shape?

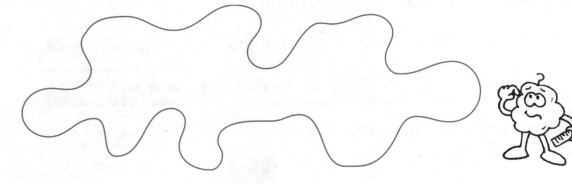

B Measure around these letters using string.

Which letter uses the **most** string? ☐

Which letter uses the **least** string? ☐

C Which would you use: **metres** or **centimetres**?

1. I would use _____ to measure a wall.

2. I would use _____ to measure the floor.

3. I would use _____ to measure my pencil.

4. I would use _____ to measure a juice-carton.

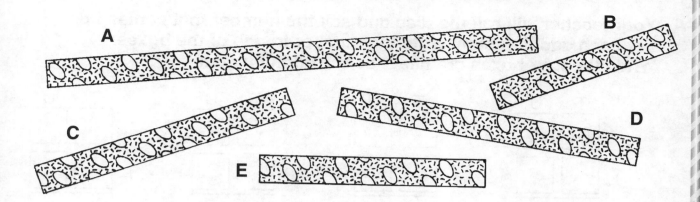

A How long are each of these bars? Estimate, then measure.

Object	Estimate	Amount
Bar A		
Bar B		
Bar C		
Bar D		
Bar E		

B

A + B = ☐ cm.   E + B = ☐ cm.

C + D = ☐ cm.   E + C = ☐ cm.

E + A = ☐ cm.   A + D + C = ☐ cm.

A + D = ☐ cm.   B + D + E = ☐ cm.

C The difference between **E** and **C** is ☐ cm.

The difference between **E** and **D** is ☐ cm.

The difference between **C** and **B** is ☐ cm.

117

A Your teacher will roll the dice and say the number that comes up.
For each addition sum, write the number in **one** of the boxes.
When the four boxes are filled, do the addition sum.

T U   T U   T U   T U

+   +   +   +

T U   T U   T U   T U

+   +   +   +

B For each sum, find out:

1. Who got the **biggest** answer?

2. Who got the **smallest** answer?

3. Who got an **even** answer?

4. Who got an **odd** answer?

C Roll the dice for subtraction sums. Remember that if the top
number is smaller than the bottom number the sum cannot be
done. **X** the sums that cannot be done.

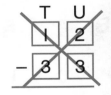

T U   T U   T U   T U

–   –   –   –

T U   T U   T U   T U

–   –   –   –

Across

2. 24 + 28 = ☐

4. 23 + ☐ = 60

6. ☐ − 16 = 15

8. 27 + 19 = ☐

10. 12 + 20 + 30 = ☐

13. 80 − 35 = ☐

15. 26 + 47 = ☐

17. ☐ + 14 = 67

19. 13 + ☐ = 41

Down

1. 30 − 17 = ☐

3. 51 − 28 = ☐

5. 37 + 37 = ☐

7. 18 + ☐ = 34

9. 47 + 17 = ☐

11. 95 − 68 = ☐

12. 49 + 28 = ☐

14. 21 + 25 + 9 = ☐

16. ☐ − 19 = 13

18. 68 − 29 = ☐

A What different coins could you use to make up a €1?

€1 = 100c

B Write the € sign.

C In these piggy banks, show 4 different ways of making up a €1.
Do not use more than 10 coins.

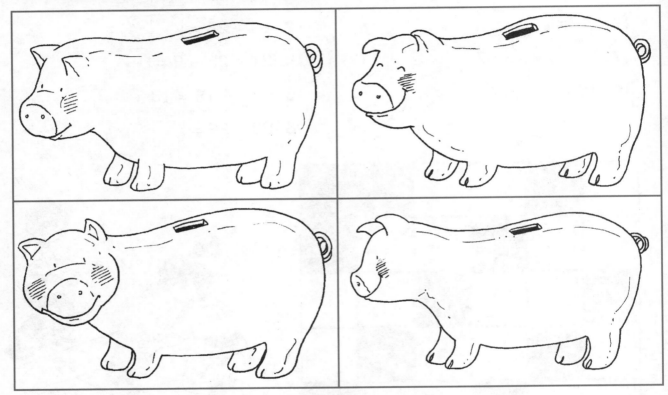

D Jessie has to put coins to the value of €1 in bags. In each bag she may only use **one type** of coin.
Write the **amount** of each coin she puts in the bags. The first one is done.

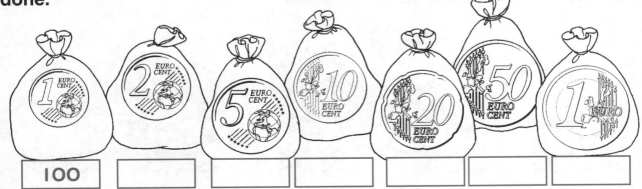

100					

A How much money is in each of these bags?

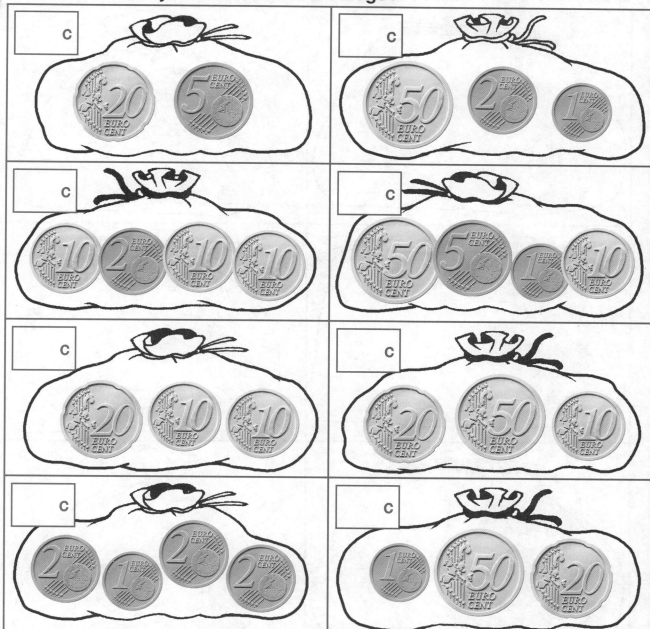

B If you have the following coins, how much do you have?

1c, 2c, 2c	_____ c	5c, 2c, 20c _____ c
5c, 10c	_____ c	10c, 5c, 5c _____ c
20c, 5c, 2c	_____ c	2c, 5c, 10c _____ c
10c, 10c, 1c	_____ c	50c, 20c, 5c _____ c
20c, 50c	_____ c	2c, 5c, 10c, 20c _____ c
50c, 20c	_____ c	5c, 5c, 1c, 2c _____ c

A Draw more coins so that the total in each purse is €2.

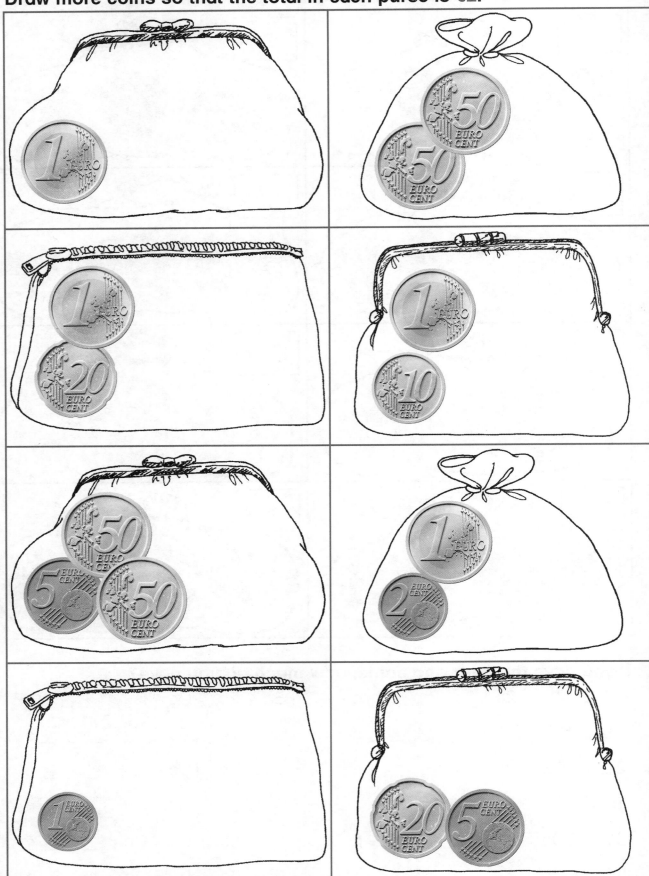

A How many €1 and 1c coins would you get for the following amounts of money?

123c,　　114c,　　142c,　　175c,　　160c,　　108c,　　110c,　　139c

> Another way of writing 100c is €1·00
> Another way of writing 135c is €1·35
> Another way of writing 103c is €1·03
> Another way of writing 20c is €0·20

B Try these.

€1·32 = 132c　　€1·61 = ____　　€1·40 = ____　　€0·07 = ____

€1·25 = ____　　€1·16 = ____　　€1·09 = ____　　€1·98 = ____

€1·87 = ____　　€1·70 = ____　　€1·12 = ____　　€0·65 = ____

€0·72 = ____　　€0·61 = ____　　€1·05 = ____　　€1·21 = ____

€0·08 = ____　　€0·90 = ____　　€0·10 = ____　　€1·31 = ____

C Try these.

126c = €1·26　　154c = ____　　178c = ____　　102c = ____

160c = ____　　181c = ____　　115c = ____　　78c = ____

107c = ____　　43c = ____　　129c = ____　　16c = ____

106c = ____　　130c = ____　　76c = ____　　34c = ____

51c = ____　　101c = ____　　81c = ____　　112c = ____

D How much was in each of these purses?

E To do at home.

Find 10 items that cost **less than** €2.

Make a list of these items and their prices.

A A group of children go to the shop.
How much does each of them spend?

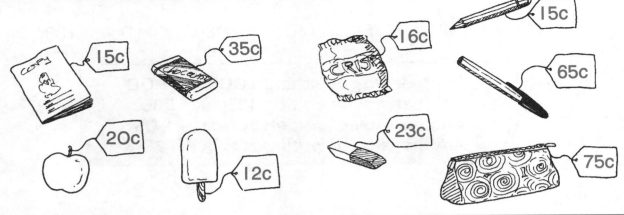

Jim		Anne		Peter	
copy	_____	pencil	_____	pencil case	_____
chocolate	_____	ice pop	_____	apple	_____
He spends:	_____	**She spends:**	_____	**He spends:**	_____
David		**Linda**		**Sandra**	
crisps	_____	pencil	_____	chocolate	_____
apple	_____	eraser	_____	apple	_____
copy	_____	ice pop	_____	eraser	_____
He spends:	_____	**She spends:**	_____	**She spends:**	_____

B What change would I get?

I have	I buy	My change
50c	copy, apple	
50c	2 ice pops, eraser	
80c	chocolate, crisps, eraser	
90c	2 copies, pencil, ice-pop, apple	

C You have 90c to spend. Make out 6 different lists of things you could buy at this shop.

Menu

SALE!

SALE!

Hamburger	35c	Cola	30c
Cheeseburger	38c	Orange Juice	28c
		Milk shake	36c
6 Chicken Nuggets	49c		
		Apple-pie	25c
Fries	27c		
		Burger Palace Pencil	9c

A Six children have €1 each to spend.
Write six different orders they could give.
How much change did each child get?
The first order is done for you.

Order 1.		Order 2.		Order 3.	
Hamburger	35c		c		c
Fries	27c		c		c
Orange Juice	28c		c		c
Total	90c	Total	c	Total	c
Change	10c	Change	c	Change	c
Order 4.		Order 5.		Order 6.	
	c		c		c
	c		c		c
	c		c		c
Total	c	Total	c	Total	c
Change	c	Change	c	Change	c

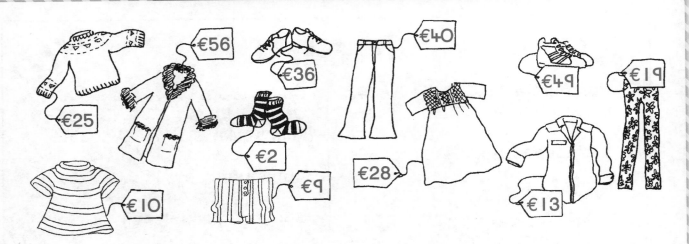

A Find the cost of:

Runners, T-shirt, leggings	€ _____	A jumper and a coat	€ _____
A jumper and trousers	€ _____	Leggings and a T-shirt	€ _____
A coat and shoes	€ _____	Shorts and trousers	€ _____
Trousers, runners, socks	€ _____	Runners, T-shirt, leggings	€ _____
Trousers, shoes, socks	€ _____	A coat, shorts, leggings	€ _____
Runners, a shirt, a dress	€ _____	Shoes, socks, leggings	€ _____

B Find the change:

From **€45** if you bought a jumper.   € _____

From **€50** if you bought shoes.   € _____

From **€60** if you bought shoes.   € _____

From **€65** if you bought trousers.   € _____

From **€80** if you bought shoes and trousers.   € _____

From **€85** if you bought a coat.   € _____

From **€90** if you bought a jumper and a coat.   € _____

C Make up your own shopping list for the clothes shop. Warning! You may not spend more than €100! What is the total cost?

A Ask each child in your class, "What is your favourite ice cream: vanilla, chocolate, mint or banana?"
Colour a box for each child you ask.

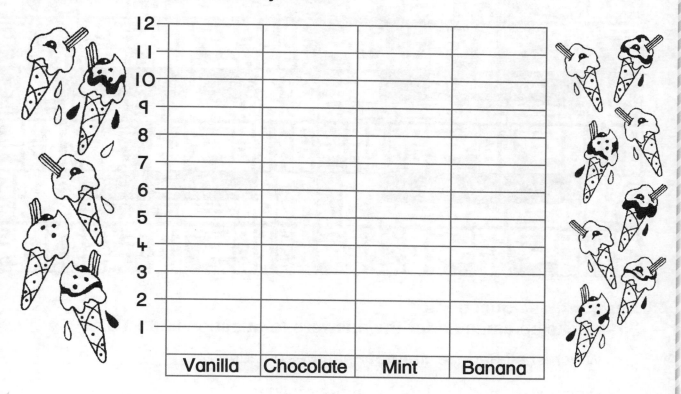

	Vanilla	Chocolate	Mint	Banana

B Answer these questions.

1. Which ice cream do **most** children prefer? _____

2. Which ice cream do **fewest** children prefer? _____

3. What is the difference between the number of children who prefer **vanilla** and the number of children who prefer **chocolate**? ____

4. What is the difference between the number of children who prefer **banana** and the number of children who prefer **mint**? _____

C Make up five questions of your own about the graph.

1. _____

2. _____

3. _____

4. _____

5. _____

Barry went to the video shop. These were the videos on the shelves:

New Releases (17)	Drama (18)
Adventure (46)	Children's (29)
Comedy (34)	Cartoons (23)

A Answer these questions.
First make an estimate for the answers to questions 3 to 10.

1. Which shelf had the **greatest** number of videos? _____

2. Which shelf had the **least** number of videos? _____

3. What is the total of **children's** videos and **cartoons**? _____

4. What is the total of **adventure** and **comedy** videos? _____

5. What is the total of **new releases** and **children's** videos? _____

6. How many more **adventure** videos are there than **cartoons**? _____

7. How many more **adventure** videos are there than **drama** videos? __

8. What is the difference between?

   a. the number of **drama** videos and **children's** videos _____

   b. the number of **comedy** videos and **cartoons** _____

9. 5 more videos were added to the new releases.
   How many videos are now on the new releases shelf? _____

10. Barry returned 2 videos to the children's shelf.
    Soon 6 videos were taken from this shelf.
    How many videos were then on the children's shelf ? _____

WEIGHT

A   Which is heavier, **A** or **B**?   ☐

Which is heavier, **C** or **D**?   ☐

What does this picture tell you about **A** and **D**?

_____

B   Write sentences using these words.

lighter than   _____

heavier than   _____

weighs the same as   _____

is the heaviest   _____

is the lightest   _____

C   Think about it.

Which is the **heaviest**?   _____

Which is the **lightest**?   _____

Weigh them and find out.
Use a balance and marbles or Base Ten units.

D   Finish these sentences.

The apple weighs the same as _____ marbles.

The lunch box weighs the same as _____ marbles.

The maths book weighs the same as _____ marbles.

The **heaviest** object is the _____.

The **lightest** object is the _____.

A

|  weighs [ ] links |  weighs [ ] crayons |  weighs [ ] Base Ten units |
|  weighs [ ] links |  weighs [ ] crayons |  weighs [ ] Base Ten units |

B Find **3** things in your lunchbox. Draw them and then weigh them.

| weighs [ ] links | weighs [ ] links | weighs [ ] links |

C Which would you choose to weigh each object. Tick ✓

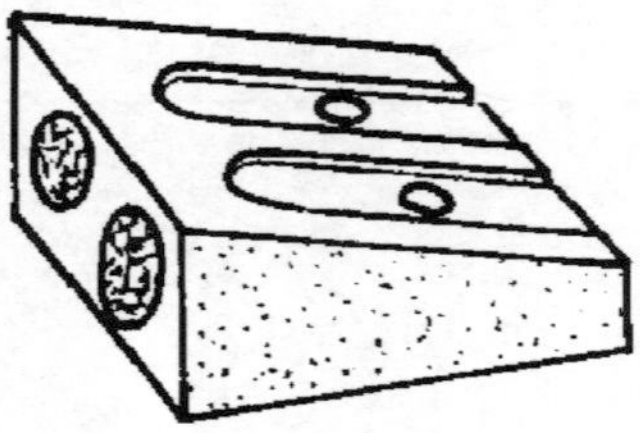

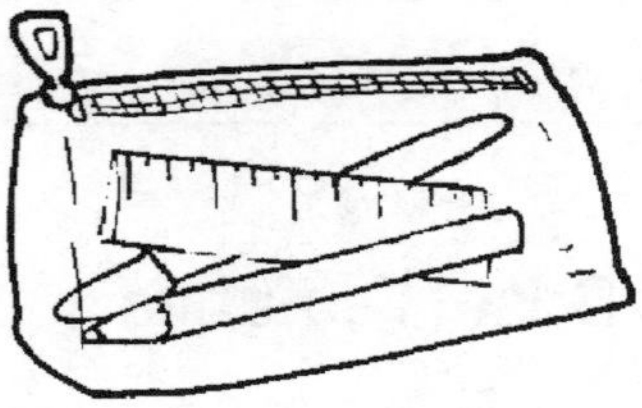

D

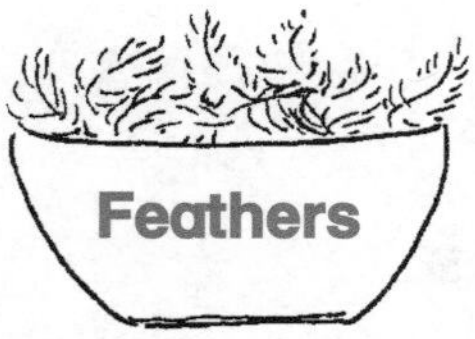

Feathers   50c coins   Links

Which is the heaviest? _____

Which is the lightest? _____

A Take an object that weighs 1 kilogramme in one hand. By balancing different objects in your other hand, find 5 objects that weigh:
about 1 kilogramme; less than 1 kilogramme.

About 1 kilogramme	Less than 1 kilogramme
1.	
2.	
3.	
4.	
5.	

B Find objects in your classroom that are: about 1 kilogramme, about $\frac{1}{2}$ kilogramme, about $\frac{1}{4}$ kilogramme.
Estimate first and then weigh the objects below. Tick the correct box.

Item	Estimate	About 1 kilogramme	About $\frac{1}{2}$ kilogramme	About $\frac{1}{4}$ kilogramme
Library book				
Shoe				
Pencil case				
Maths book				
Copy				
Reader				
Lunch box				

C To do at home.
Find 3 objects that weigh 1 kilogramme (1 kg), 3 objects that weigh $\frac{1}{2}$ kilogramme and 3 objects that weigh $\frac{1}{4}$ kilogramme.

A Write number sentences and find the answers. Use a 100 square, a number line or Base Ten blocks to help you. You may be able to work some of them out in your head.

Find the difference between **50** and **23**. ___50 – 23___ ☐

Find the difference between **61** and **33**. _____ ☐

Find the difference between **75** and **39**. _____ ☐

B What number is **24** more than **32**? _____ ☐

What number is **17** more than **19**? _____ ☐

What number is **27** more than **43**? _____ ☐

C What number is **12** less than **43**? _____ ☐

What number is **20** less than **67**? _____ ☐

What number is **18** less than **51**? _____ ☐

What number is **29** less than **83**? _____ ☐

D What number must be added to **34** to reach **49**? _____ ☐

What number must be added to **15** to reach **41**? _____ ☐

What number must be added to **40** to reach **68**? _____ ☐

What number must be added to **48** to reach **72**? _____ ☐

E Take **14** from **75** _____ ☐   Take **18** from **67** _____ ☐

Take **13** from **56** _____ ☐   Take **39** from **52** _____ ☐

Take **32** from **90** _____ ☐   Take **24** from **80** _____ ☐

F 1. Pam had **19** computer games. She got **5** more. How many has she now? _____ ☐

2. Mary had **43** sheets of notepaper. She gave **16** sheets to her sister. How many has she left? _____ ☐

A Fill in the frames.

6	3	4	8	2	7	9	5
+ ☐	+ ☐	+ ☐	+ ☐	+ ☐	+ ☐	+ ☐	+ ☐
8	7	10	16	5	8	12	12

5	4	6	3	6	8	7	9
+ ☐	+ ☐	+ ☐	+ ☐	+ ☐	+ ☐	+ ☐	+ ☐
10	8	14	13	9	12	16	17

B Now try these.

2 2	3 1	2 5	6 3	4 5	3 6
+ ☐	+ ☐	+ ☐	+ ☐	+ ☐	+ ☐
3 6	5 6	4 8	7 8	8 9	8 9

6 8	2 5	6 3	4 5	3 4	5 6
+ ☐	+ ☐	+ ☐	+ ☐	+ ☐	+ ☐
8 3	5 0	6 5	5 3	7 1	6 4

C Fill in the frames. Can you find an easy way to do them?

☐	☐	☐	☐	☐	☐	☐	☐	☐
− 6	− 4	− 4	− 3	− 3	− 5	− 1	− 0	− 4
3	2	1	4	6	3	5	8	0

D Now try these.

☐	☐	☐	☐	☐	☐
− 1 4	− 3 2	− 2 3	− 1 5	− 3 6	− 4 3
3 1	2 6	2 1	2 9	3 6	2 7

☐	☐	☐	☐	☐	☐
− 1 6	− 2 9	− 3 7	− 4 4	− 5 6	− 6 4
2 4	1 8	1 2	3 1	1 9	1 0

A Here are some objects that turn. Make a list of other objects that turn. Draw them in your copy.

 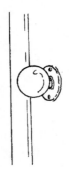 

B Look at these circles. Colour the turns. One is done.

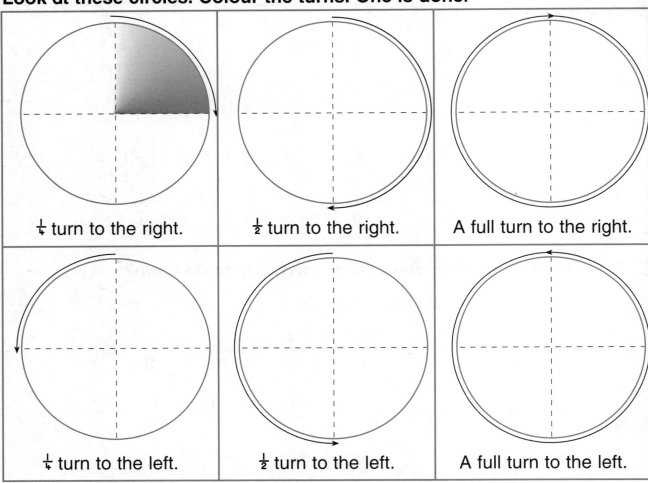

¼ turn to the right. ½ turn to the right. A full turn to the right.

¼ turn to the left. ½ turn to the left. A full turn to the left.

C P Fold a circle in quarters like this:

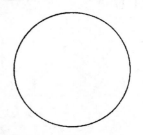  

This is a **square corner**. Which turn is it like above?

 turn

A   Look around the classroom. Can you see any square corners?
Check with the square corner you have made.

B   **List 5 objects that have a square corner.**

   1. _____

   2. _____

   3. _____

   4. _____

   5. _____

C   **Which 3-D shapes have square corners? Tick (✓) the correct box.**

The **cube** has square corners. ☐

The **cube** has no square corners. ☐

The **sphere** has square corners. ☐

The **sphere** has no square corners. ☐

The **cone** has square corners. ☐

The **cone** has no square corners. ☐

D   **How many square corners does a cuboid have?** _____

E   **Look for square corners at home. List 9 of them here.**

  1. _____   4. _____   7. _____

  2. _____   5. _____   8. _____

  3. _____   6. _____   9. _____

A Fill in the missing numbers.

5 + 3 = ☐   8 + ☐ = 14   10 + ☐ = 3 + 10

9 + 2 = ☐   ☐ + 6 = 13   8 = 4 + ☐

10 + 7 = ☐   8 + 3 + ☐ = 17   11 − 2 = ☐

6 + 6 = ☐   5 + 4 = 4 + ☐   15 − 8 = ☐

7 + 5 + 7 = ☐   2 + 6 = ☐ + 2   7 − ☐ = 2

B Fill in the missing signs: + − = < >

5 ☐ 2 + 3   4 ☐ 7   9 ☐ 4 + 4

5 ☐ 8 = 13   10 ☐ 2 = 8   9 ☐ 0 = 9

C

2 7	3 2	5 0	3 7	5 9	4 5
+ 4 1	+ 3 4	+ 3 6	+ 4	+ 1 8	+ 2 5

5 4	6 1	4 6	9 4	8 1	4 3
+ 2 0	+ 2 9	+ 4 8	+ 4	+ 9	+ 3 9

2 3	1 2	2 4	1 6	2 7	4 3
1 4	6 6	1 2	2 5	1 6	2 9
+ 3	+ 8	+ 3 3	+ 4	+ 1 5	+ 2 4

D

4 5	8 7	6 3	5 1	9 0	7 3
− 1 3	− 4 2	− 2 0	− 2 4	− 4 7	− 1 9

3 8	6 4	4 5	7 0	8 2	4 5
− 2 9	− 2 8	− 3 2	− 4 3	− 6 0	− 3 8

A Finish these patterns.

11, 12, 13, ☐, ☐, ☐, ☐ 96, 97, ☐, ☐, ☐, ☐, ☐

125, 126, ☐, ☐, ☐ 32, 34, 36, ☐, ☐, ☐, ☐

0, 3, 6, ☐, ☐, ☐, ☐ 0, 10, 20, ☐, ☐, ☐, ☐

B Here are the answers to some subtraction sums.
Write a sum for each answer.

☐ − ☐ = 3   ☐ − ☐ = 7   ☐ − ☐ = 10

☐ − ☐ = 5   ☐ − ☐ = 8   ☐ − ☐ = 1

☐ − ☐ = 2   ☐ − ☐ = 4   ☐ − ☐ = 9

C What time do these clocks show?

_____ _____ _____ _____

D Write these times in digital time.

_____ _____ _____ _____

A What numbers are shown on the place-value boards?

B Colour $\frac{1}{2}$ of this shape.   Colour $\frac{1}{4}$ of this shape.

C There were 16 sweets in a packet.
Anne ate $\frac{1}{2}$ of them.   Jim ate $\frac{1}{4}$ of them.   Karen ate $\frac{1}{4}$ of them.

1. How many sweets did Anne eat? _____

2. How many sweets did Jim eat? _____

3. How many sweets did Karen eat? _____

4. How many sweets were left? _____

D Colour the square blue, the triangle yellow, the rectangle green, the oval brown, and the circle red.

A Look at these 3-D shapes: a cube, a cone, a sphere, a cuboid.

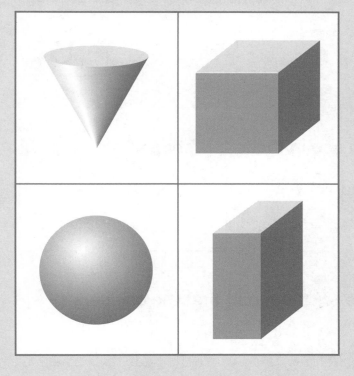

1. What 3-D shape is in the top right corner?

_____

2. What 3-D shape is in the bottom left corner?

_____

3. What 3-D shape is under the cube?

_____

4. What 3-D shape is above and to the left of the cuboid?

_____

B Here are the names of some measuring units:

centimetre   metre   kilogramme   litre

Which unit would you use:

1. to measure the length of a classroom? _____

2. to measure the amount of water in a bucket? _____

3. to weigh a sack of potatoes? _____

4. to measure the length of a pencil? _____

5. to measure the length of a field? _____

6. to measure the amount of lemonade in a bottle? _____

C Peter's uncle gave him 95c. He went to the shop and bought a bar for 35c and an apple for 18c. How much change did he get from the 95c?

139

A List these items in order from heaviest to lightest.

matchstick   copy   feather   school bag

1. _____   2. _____   3. _____   4. _____

B Tick the square corners that you see in these 2-D shapes.

C Here are some word sentences.
Can you write number sentences for them and find the answers?

1. There are **8** sweets in a pack.
   How many are there in **3** packs?
   ☐ + ☐ + ☐ = ☐
2. A bar costs **5c**.
   How much for **3** bars?
   ☐ + ☐ + ☐ = ☐
3. One rabbit has **2** ears.
   How many have **7** rabbits?
   ☐ + ☐ + ☐ + ☐ + ☐ + ☐ + ☐ = ☐
4. A table has **4** legs.
   How many legs have **4** tables?
   ☐ + ☐ + ☐ + ☐ = ☐
5. **3** lollipop sticks make **1** triangle.
   How many will make **6** triangles?
   ☐ + ☐ + ☐ + ☐ + ☐ + ☐ = ☐

D Fill in this addition square.

+	3	1	5	8	2	9	0	4	10	7
10										
5										
8										
0										
3										
7										
9										
1										
6										
4										

A Across

1. Find the difference between 50 and 23.
3. What number is 17 more than 19?
4. What number is 29 less than 83?
7. 19 plus 19.
8. Take 39 from 54.
9. What number must be added to 40 to make 68?
12. What number is 18 less than 44?

Down

1. Add 13 and 12.
2. What number must be added to 6 to make 80?
3. Take 50 from 87.
5. Find the difference between 33 and 61.
6. What number must be added to 34 to make 49?
7. 70 minus 40.
8. Find the difference between 12 and 30.
9. What number is 29 less than 56?
10. Add 36 and 40.
11. Take 32 from 90.

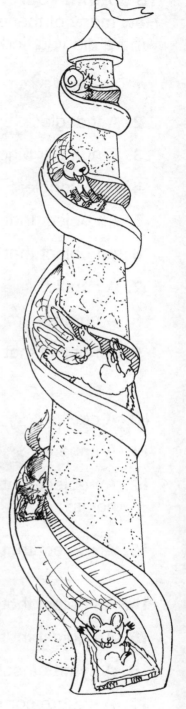

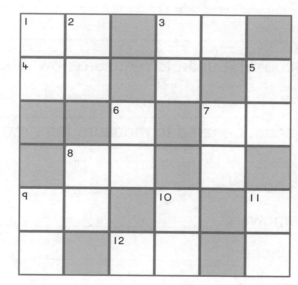

B When you know these, colour them in your addition square or subtraction grid.

$$5 + 3 = 8 \qquad 8 - 5 = 3 \qquad 8 - 3 = 5$$

To do with your friend.
How many of these objects can you find in the classroom?
Where did you find each one?

 1. A cube: _____

 2. A triangle: _____

 3. A number bigger than 100: _____

 4. A rectangle: _____

 5. An object that could be used to tell the time: _____

 6. An object that could be used to tell the date: _____

 7. A cuboid: _____

 8. A number smaller than 20: _____

 9. An object that could be used to measure the length of the classroom:

 _____

10. A circle: _____

11. A sphere: _____

12. An object that could be used to measure how much liquid a container holds:

 _____

13. An object that could be used to measure the area of your table:

 _____

14. An object that shows $\frac{1}{2}$: _____

15. An object that shows $\frac{1}{4}$: _____

16. A symmetrical shape: _____

17. A square corner: _____

18. An object that measures about 1 cm : _____

19. An object that measures about 1 m : _____

20. An object that weighs about 1 kg : _____

Number of objects you found: [ ]

P

+	0	1	2	3	4	5	6	7	8	9	10
0	0	1	2	3	4	5	6	7	8	9	10
1	1	2	3	4	5	6	7	8	9	10	11
2	2	3	4	5	6	7	8	9	10	11	12
3	3	4	5	6	7	8	9	10	11	12	13
4	4	5	6	7	8	9	10	11	12	13	14
5	5	6	7	8	9	10	11	12	13	14	15
6	6	7	8	9	10	11	12	13	14	15	16
7	7	8	9	10	11	12	13	14	15	16	17
8	8	9	10	11	12	13	14	15	16	17	18
9	9	10	11	12	13	14	15	16	17	18	19
10	10	11	12	13	14	15	16	17	18	19	20

Remember:

If you know 7 + 3
you know 3 + 7.

If you know 9 + 6
you know 6 + 9.

P

−	0	1	2	3	4	5	6	7	8	9	10
20											10
19										10	9
18									10	9	8
17								10	9	8	7
16							10	9	8	7	6
15						10	9	8	7	6	5
14					10	9	8	7	6	5	4
13				10	9	8	7	6	5	4	3
12			10	9	8	7	6	5	4	3	2
11		10	9	8	7	6	5	4	3	2	1
10	10	9	8	7	6	5	4	3	2	1	0
9	9	8	7	6	5	4	3	2	1	0	
8	8	7	6	5	4	3	2	1	0		
7	7	6	5	4	3	2	1	0			
6	6	5	4	3	2	1	0				
5	5	4	3	2	1	0					
4	4	3	2	1	0						
3	3	2	1	0							
2	2	1	0								
1	1	0									
0	0										

144